The
Magdalene
Frequency

The Magdalene Frequency

Become the Love You Are,
Not the Love You Seek

A Sacred Planet Book

ADELE VENNERI

Translated by Susanna Memoli

Bear & Company
Rochester, Vermont

Bear & Company
One Park Street
Rochester, Vermont 05767
www.BearandCompanyBooks.com

Bear & Company is a division of Inner Traditions International

Sacred Planet Books are curated by Richard Grossinger, Inner Traditions editorial board member and cofounder and former publisher of North Atlantic Books. The Sacred Planet collection, published under the umbrella of the Inner Traditions family of imprints, includes works on the themes of consciousness, cosmology, alternative medicine, dreams, climate, permaculture, alchemy, shamanic studies, oracles, astrology, crystals, hyperobjects, locutions, and subtle bodies.

Cataloging-in-Publication Data for this title is available from the Library of Congress

ISBN 978-1-59143-500-6 (print)
ISBN 978-1-59143-501-3 (ebook)

Printed and bound in the United States by Lake Book Manufacturing, LLC

10   9   8   7   6   5   4   3   2   1

Text design and layout by Virginia Scott Bowman
This book was typeset in Garamond Premier Pro and Gill Sans with Nexa and Roxborough used as the display typefaces

To send correspondence to the author of this book, mail a first-class letter to the author c/o Inner Traditions • Bear & Company, One Park Street, Rochester, VT 05767, and we will forward the communication, or contact the author directly at **www.adelevenneri.com**.

To You, my Soul
who with deep Passion
have lived with me
all my infinite Existences.
To You, Eternal Spirit
from whom everything Originated.
To You, Pioneer of an Eternal Consciousness.
To You, Divine-Human.

The Code of the Origin by Adele Venneri.

Adele Venneri, Rennes-le-Château, France.
Photo by Stefano Scrimieri.

Contents

Foreword

The first consideration you will make as you begin to read this book will be to have the feeling that it was written for you.

But you, not as a woman or a man.

No. By you I mean YOU who have the book in your hands at this moment.

The words of Magdalene, so wonderfully channeled by Adele in a poetical form at times, are addressed to each soul with such powerful strength that it leaves one surprised, astonished. The frequency that arrives is very strong, like a laser, and is capable of going beyond.

Every sentence was written for YOU.

Every concept awakens in YOU a distant memory.

Every invitation is a warning, so that YOU can transform your life.

Every incitement overwhelms you with Divine Enthusiasm, Divine Joy, Divine Awakening.

That is what happened to me. Sometimes I was so impressed by what I was reading that I would ask Adele if the text she had sent me was part of the book or whether it was a message uniquely for me.

Once, during one of those days where things go a bit wrong, I decided to stop. I lit a candle and also a nice incense to try to relax. With a vehemence and urgency to know, I asked my guides to present themselves and tell me what was happening to me. The phone rang, interrupting my questions; my intuition told me to answer. On the other side was Adele— actually it was Magdalene, because it was she who told Adele to call me exactly in that instant. With sweet firmness, without any pause, Adele read me the message she had just channeled. Amazement, emotion. I cannot describe in words what I felt.

"If you feel strong in asserting I'm a doctor, ask yourself, 'Who Am I without a white coat?' If you feel strong in asserting I'm a teacher, ask yourself, 'Who Am I without a desk?'" These are some of the words that entered directly into my heart. In a moment when I was having problems with my publishing house, SHE invited me to go out of my role as publisher and writer and she invited me to feel MY SOUL.

Dear reader, this will happen to YOU as well. It will be sufficient to read the first pages, and you will have the sensation that the frequency of Mary Magdalene knows you more than anyone else. Through what she says, she indicates how you can transform your life and let go of the obsolete habits and certainties of the old world that is dying so that the New Time can be born with the enthusiasm of pure love.

On Magdalene I have read dozens of books. I myself have written about Magdalene, and I continue to write books to foster spiritual awakening. Yet I have never experienced such a strong emotion, which reached directly into my heart and left me without breath.

This book is a hymn to Love in all its forms, but above all it is a penetrating guide, never strict, that brings us the truth about the pure love between Myriam and Yeshua. Not so much on a historical level, but rather to reveal to us that it is through the transparency of their Union that the awakening of the feminine in balance with the masculine inside each one of us expresses itself. The Eternal Consciousness of Mary Magdalene pervades Earth, and it shows to us how to transform ourselves and the entire planet.

I love Magdalene!

I love her deeply, and for years I have been following her steps on Earth.

SHE talks to my heart.

I will surprise you right away: for some time I have been convinced that I first began to love her at the time of the Essenes and have followed her on her journey to Gaul. I do not know if this is reality or fantasy. What I do know is that—as Magdalene herself revealed to me—I have loved her in every woman I have met in various lifetimes.

I have felt her so many times up and down the streets of France, even recently in Rennes-le-Château, where I have been with Adele and other friends. I worshipped her in the Templar cathedrals of France and in Vézelay, to make—as Adele writes—the two parts of me fall in love, my masculine and my feminine, to become the ONE of the Sacred Androgyny.

I have always loved her, especially now, because in this new book she talks to us with sweetness and firmness, and many truths that I have felt in my heart for a long time come out. Myriam invites us to let go of Christ on the cross, that icon of suffering and drama, and release a new and bursting energy that forever removes him from the cross. Enough with suffering and with its symbols on Earth. The religious authorities falsely called Myriam a prostitute to conceal not only her but all women, depriving them of their dignity, and also all men, from whom the inner feminine part was ripped off, leading them to look for it outside (as happened to me).

Ignoring her relationship with Yeshua, for whom Magdalene was the first of the Apostles, was the most insidious way to propagate a religion built on rational power, excluding feminine creativity.

Magdalene is the other half of Christ and will return to be worshipped at the altars of the New Religion, which is that of Love. This is the New Time.

It is not up to me, now, to anticipate the many teachings that Magdalene gave to Adele, because you can taste and feel them, page after page.

We have to reconstitute in us the Sacred Androgyny, which is not something sexual, but is the way to reach the full Union of our masculine aspect with the feminine one and of our soul with the Universal Creative Spirit.

We must be able to transform the old energy in the New Energy, the pain in time of Joy. This is what Christ came to give us. What God has always wanted for us human beings. As Magdalene says: *"I'm neither a male nor a female. I am the Kristic Union that is within you."*

"In the Eternal Consciousness of Me," says Magdalene again, "there is no past to suffer for, but there is a Present with which to Create."

We must transform the past so that we all recognize God within ourselves.

This is one of the new teachings that all Masters of the Spirit are making known on Earth, certainly referring to a historical past but also to our personal past. We must concretely act, transforming and letting go of the old things around us, forgiving us and forgiving those who are enemies, dissolving the weight of an ancient karma.

These are words that enter us like a continuous flow of Waves of Love that excite us, move us, give meaning to our daily life.

The words bring back ancient memories. And that is why every word, every concept that Magdalene brings to us makes us rejoice because at last we see brought to Light all that the religious authorities had concealed from us, which now bursts forth forcefully in our hearts.

We inhale the scent of these Truths. We feel their essence.

We feel joy and infinite love because thanks to the messages given to Adele, Magdalene can manifest herself in all Her Greatness as a Goddess, as the most perfect and sacred bearer of the Love message of the Cosmic Union between Myriam and Yeshua.

Thanks to her Eternal Consciousness the time for Change and for Transformation has finally come, the Time of the New has finally come. Letting go completely to the Eternal, to the Eternal Consciousness of Magdalene, this is it.

It is time to let go, to trust your intuition, your own heart that knows all the Truths.

Thank you Magdalene, for your words. Thanks. I thank Adele and Magdalene for choosing me to write this foreword. The request to write it is a further proof of the love that Magdalene has for me.

And YOU who are reading remember. This is a book written for YOU, and it can really transform your life completely.

I conclude with Magdalene's words:

"The New Time is NOW. The New Time is PRESENCE. . . . The Eternal Consciousness is NOW.

I love you, soul companion, I love You deeply . . .

In the name of the Rose, so it is."

GIAN MARCO BRAGADIN, MILANO, JANUARY 17, 2016.

GIAN MARCO BRAGADIN, the author of more than 30 works, editor, spiritual researcher, and avid spiritual traveler has been called "the last Templar." He founded *Melchisedek Edizioni* Publishing House and has written historical-esoteric novels. A media and advertising expert, he also worked in radio and co-authored several television shows. He created the science of "*SegniAnalisi*" (SignAnalysis). He is known as the first popularizer of the figure of Mary Magdalene in Italy.

Translator's Preface

*T*ranslating this book was the most cathartic experience of my life.

On March 11, 2020, while the world was stopping because of the coronavirus pandemic, I happily attended a conference in Montserrat, Spain, with Adele Venneri. In that sacred and intimate meeting, she expressed her wish to see one of her books translated into English. Without hesitation I chose to undertake this initiatory journey and to finally give light to this creation.

To explain, though, how it all started and why I embarked on such a journey, I must go back to January 2019 when I first received this alchemical book as a gift from a friend. I read it in Italian all in one go. Everything resonated deeply with me and tears of emotion flowed, as I realized this was not a book like the others I had read about Mary Magdalene.

With great pleasure and excitement I decided to meet Adele Venneri on July 22, 2019, during an experiential holiday to celebrate Mary Magdalene at Rennes-le-Château. A very charismatic and generous woman, she with great mastery and presence radiated her frequency, reawakening mine.

As an anthropologist, passionate about the sacred femi-nine, I had investigated this topic for years looking for answers outside me. This book, on the other hand, invited me to search for answers within myself where my truth lies. It is a book that speaks about love, self-love. It is a book that speaks to me about myself, directly to my heart with a simple yet powerful language because it is imbued with the frequency of love, the frequency of the origin, which reminds me who I am every time I read it.

I had the privilege afterward to take two powerful and intense paths of self-awareness with Adele Venneri, who with gentle firmness brought me home, to me. I had several trans-mutations by simply observing aspects of me that required my attention, bringing them home and unifying myself. I gave birth to myself with a new consciousness, becoming aware that I am the love I have always looked for and I am the creator of and responsible for my life.

I smile thinking how everything is perfect and how all my life experiences, apparently disconnected and not worthy of notice, became instead very useful tools for me to embark on this amazing experience.

Having a Spanish mother, I lived in Spain, and I worked as a translator of European licenses and marks for D'Agostini Organizzazione S.L. For other personal reasons, I also lived in Brisbane, Australia, for ten years, and that is why I speak fluent English and I could translate this amazing book.

I started this wonderful yet unknown journey of trans-lating the frequency of Mary Magdalene, aware it would be profound and intense just like the other experiences I have had, thanks to the author and the carrier of this frequency, but I did not know yet how and what it would be like. I was about to find out, and my goodness, I can say now it has indeed been quite a remarkable and unimaginable journey that shook me to the core.

During the translating experience, I have learned to combine my rational with my intuitive side, giving light to this wonderful creation. I began using only my intuition, trusting my English knowledge was sufficient. Thus, my masculine side came to cooperate with the feminine side, choosing the appropriate word and sound.

In the process of translating, I became more aware, with great astonishment, that the English language is androgynous because it does not have feminine and masculine endings like the Italian and Spanish languages. Thus, I feel that it is the ideal language to unify. Perhaps it is not a coincidence that nowadays it is the most-spoken language in the world, if we include non-native speakers.

As per my personal experience, I would like to highlight that although I have read this book in Italian and in Spanish many times, whenever I read it, it is always like the first time. As the author affirms, this is because it has many levels of reading. As my awareness changes, so does my understanding of it. Indeed, it is through my personal experience that I acquire awareness, and thus each I time I read it, the sound of this book resonates deeper within me. Its meaning becomes clearer and reveals profound truths to me, when I am ready and in perfect synchronicity. This is why reading it is one thing; feeling its frequency is yet another. Translating it was a real cathartic experience. It allowed me to pause, to feel every sound closer, and to go deeper inside myself, beginning a centripetal journey to my center I could never have imagined.

Chapter after chapter, I lived my experiences in my daily life. I had my ups and downs, becoming aware that only by entering my waters and observing my emotions can I really transmute my life. Indeed, I had to hit the bottom and went through the darkest night of my soul, as I was about to translate the final chapter. I finally understood what Concrete Spirituality is, which Adele Venneri talks about in her various conferences and meetings.

Thanks to this deep experience of translating, I began to feel real love and compassion for myself, understanding that there is nothing wrong about me and I am just acquiring awareness and therefore wisdom through my experiences. For a long time I have feared, judged, and denied my shadow. I did not realize I was separating myself. As Adele Venneri affirms, the shadow is the most beautiful part of ourselves. This opened my heart wide, and it was pure joy when at last I embraced my shadow, unifying myself once more.

I experienced looking at myself and recognizing myself in the mirror. It was a very intense process. It brought me home to myself and to a deeper and more intimate connection with my soul, my faithful companion. I have faith in myself: I am listening to myself, my inner voice, and following the dictates of my soul. This is the greatest gift I have given myself, the fruit of my profound transmutation.

I am honored to have had this opportunity to translate

Adele Venneri's book, which in reality is much more than a book. It is a portal that has offered me the most fabulous journey of my life, going deeper to the center of myself and to connect intimately with my soul. It is a great gift the author gives to humanity, it is the key to find the way home, for those who are ready and choose do so and vibrate with the frequency of love and the origin.

I do not have words to thank Adele Venneri, except what I know best, it touches the heart in a very simple and natural way, through a deep embrace and looking into each other's eyes. In her mirror I recognized my soul, and I am forever grateful.

I wish you, dear reader, a wonderful inner journey that will surely amaze you and, if you so wish, also set you free.

SUSANNA MEMOLI

SUSANNA MEMOLI is a professional translator, fluent in four languages, a frequent traveller and passionate researcher about the cult of the Great Mother practiced by the first gilanic societies. She has dedicated a lot of time into investigating the sacred feminine and in particular, the history and figure of Mary Magdalene, seeking to learn about the feminine power that has been suppressed for millennia. Her research led her to the books of Adele Venneri, finally understanding that the inner search and the self-awareness are the key to the human evolution.

About the Language in This Book

This work faithfully reflects the message of Myriam that the author channeled to write this book. Myriam expresses herself with a new language, transformative and transmuting, which, with sweet firmness, accompanies and guides the reader toward the revelation of the book's cryptographic code. In writing the book, poetic license has been taken in word treatments—such as liberal and unusual use of capitalization, mixing capital and lowercase letters in one word (KRISTal), and using alternate spellings of words (Krist for Christ)—with the sole purpose of bringing the reader closer to Myriam's original message in its purest and deepest state.

The reader is sometimes addressed as Master and also as soul companion. When speaking of Divine-Humans (all humans, including the reader), the pronouns he, him, and his are used, but readers of all genders are intended. The word *Ray* refers to the Ray of Mary Magdalene, her frequency. Likewise, the cover artwork, *Alter Ego* by Manuela Da Ponte, done in 2010 and commissioned by Osvaldo Pirra, represents the essence of the Magdalene Frequency, as channeled through Adele Venneri. The painting was rendered with earth and salt on wood and finished with silver leaf and rosewood mineral pigment.

In addition to Myriam, key to the narrative are two protagonists: Yeshua and Joy. Yeshua is the Divine Masculine aspect who unites with Myriam in the Hieros Gamos, the cosmic marriage. Joy is the main character who embarks on an alchemical journey. By the end, the reader realizes that he or she is Joy, the person who traveled and lived this inner journey throughout the book.

Introduction

These thirteen chapters invite you to enter eight circular rooms. Here you encounter the feminine and masculine archetypes, each with its own frequency. Transmuting frequencies vibrate within you as a Mirror of the same Matrix, the creating matrix through which the Universe has created itself and the Creator self-creates.

The Magdalene Frequency is not only the title of the book that you have in your hands. The Magdalene Frequency is the Eternal Consciousness of Mary Magdalene intended not only as a historical figure that lived next to Christ two thousand years ago, but also as a vital essence, useful and essential to the Integration of the Consciousness.

The Magdalene Frequency is the *anima mundi* that generates the Universe.

The Vibratory Frequency of the Creating Origin. The archetype of the Incarnated Mastery that unifies, receives, and, like an alchemist, blends in his *cup* the elements of which the same Universe is composed: fire, air, water, and earth. The archaic priestess is present in every myth.

This book was first published in April 2016. Today,

seven years later, honored by the myriad of testimonies that I have received from my readers, I'm very glad to publish this new edition.

In the pages of this book you will not find the story or the pseudo story of Mary Magdalene that during the centuries has been made up and altered, depending on the historical context or on the needs and interests of those who were writing. Mary Magdalene is a controversial figure, concealed and vilified by the *occult power of the church* with the goal of keeping hidden not only the secrets about who she really was, but also hiding the secrets of the history of humanity.

Here it is that Mary Magdalene ceased being a great master and became the prostitute. Here it is that the beloved of Christ collapsed into the abyss of the ocean. Yet as it is known, the truth always comes out, and this truth manifests through the sound of her name, signaling her origin.

MyriaM—a name that begins and terminates with the letter M, the most sacred letter in which the masculine and feminine are attuned. Through the vocalization of the letter's sound, the power of water, and the strength of the sea is invoked.

The truth always comes out because, regardless of his acts, a man cannot SEPARATE what God unites.

When I speak of God, I do not speak of a Divine being in the celestial skies judging the living and the dead. I speak of the Unified Consciousness that generates and regulates the entire Universe through its forms, its colors, and above all its *sound*. This triad is called LOVE. But it is not the love you have been looking for in the other for centuries. It is not the love you have always nourished yourself with by drawing on the other. It is not the love you have always projected and sought in Christ, in Magdalene, or in any other entity. It is the love that YOU ARE.

As you make your way into the depths of these pages, you will discover that you are beginning an *initiatory journey* that will lead you toward You. Not to the Divine outside YOU. To you who are Human and Divine. You will feel the *frequency of Myriam,* and with this frequency, you will resonate with and enter into contact with the Magdalene that LIVES inside You, not with the Magdalene that you have always sought.

In these last years, rivers of ink have been spilled about the story of Mary Magdalene. As often happens around so much talking, the phenomenon of Mary Magdalene was created. A phenomenon that, if observed carefully in its soul matrix, arises from the urgent need of the human to regain possession of its feminine part, an essential part without which the *creation* of one's own life remains incomplete. It is thanks to the incompleteness of the self that the phenomenon of Mary Magdalene has spread, moving away from the essence of its frequency. The inner blindness of the dormant believer once more has turned his search outside himself, first searching for a Divine male, then searching for a Divine female. Both searches result from projecting a lack of self and from a lack of awareness of the force of love that, as Dante used to say, "moves the sun and the other stars."

The truth about the origin of Mary Magdalene will help you not only to know the story of a GREAT WOMAN, of a GREAT MASTER, but it will allow you to know YOUR story. It will allow you to live YOUR *mystical wedding*. Although the linear mind will try to rationalize, postulating exhaustive answers about dates and details, the truth will resonate inside you. The truth is inherent in the memory of your cells, where the frequency of Mary Magdalene is ALIVE.

Hungrily seeking to know the story of Mary Magdalene, without being curious about your own story, creates a centrifugal movement that separates what urges you to unite from what you seek, which is the inner you, the Divine-Human. This union can only happen through an intimate and personal path of awareness. Knowledge without consciousness is null. Research alone will engender even more negative feelings toward those who have continued to conceal the truth. There is no need. Harsh spirits create even harsher ones. In this epochal moment, it is urgent to return to oneself. It is urgent to meet oneself, not to go against someone.

You cannot be with the other if you miss Yourself.

In the Time of Creation in which, today, the Divine-Human finds himself experiencing the UNION, it is urgent to comprehend who and what Mary Magdalene is for YOU.

What and who represents inside of you. Exploring yourself with gentle grace, you will discover that Mary Magdalene is your own soul. She is your own consciousness. She is the creative part of you with which TO CREATE your own life. She is the soul that from the origin of times asks to be EMBODIED and no longer sought after or IDOLIZED.

In the Origin, everything was whole, everything was complete, everything was United.

The Eternal Consciousness of Mary Magdalene is Concrete Spirituality applied in everyday life, in practical experiences, not only in a group through which one satisfies his own "need of belonging" or of "recognition."

This *initiatory journey* will invite you to celebrate your alchemical marriage through which the Mystical Rose will blossom in the center of your chest.

Mary Magdalene is not only a figure from the past.

Magdalene is PRESENCE.

Magdalene is ETERNAL.

Mary Magdalene is alive, she never died.

In the name of the Rose, so it is.

1

Incipit

"*I return to unite with him, not to replace him.*" It is with this message that Myriam's Love began to talk to me. It is with these words that in the pain of the separation from myself, with Gentle Grace and Sweet Firmness, she blew into my heart consecrating me to the Sacred Union. Dressed in white with the Holy Grail at the height of her chest, she guarded in the tabernacle of my heart the Cosmic Union. She baptized me with the water of my own tears, and in the womb of the Great Mother she awakened in me my Mastery.

In the next pages I will talk to you of how my encounter with her happened, probably many words will resonate with you. Beyond the fact that you are a man or a woman, maybe in your deepest self you too have felt many times the lack of that feminine part that two thousand years ago was torn from you.

As you allow yourself to let yourself go to your feelings,

the flow of Myriam's Love will begin to flow through your Sacred Blood, reminding you of who you Are: You Are What You Are.

And who is Myriam?

Myriam is the one who has always been introduced to you by the name of Mary Magdalene.

She is the one who through the collective imagination arrived to you like a penitent, a prostitute, and a sinner. She who has historically been depicted as a symbol of the woman who sells her body, who suffers under male power. She has for centuries been gagged, through the power of those who wear the church's black dress precisely concealing the purity of the Female Kristic Seed. The religious authorities have hidden in a closet the living skeletons of those who have profoundly loved her. By gagging her, the Creative Mother of the Divine-Human has been silenced, the Sacred Feminine aspect capable of *creating* its own life.

The story of Magdalene began long before the time of her beloved Yeshua. It was born with the Mother Goddess at the origin of life itself. At the beginning, her presence was irrefutable, her Spirit unique and absolute.

Then it happened that the Divine-Human began to feel *homesick,* and that's how the *journey* began, thanks to which, life after life, he discovered within himself what he was looking for outside. His consciousness, still too young, forgot his Divine nature, projecting outside himself the presence of a multitude of gods. Tired of what he had created himself, he unified the faith in a unique Male God, forgetting the Goddess that had always existed. Religions were born, and every one made use of the right God, and here it is that the confusion between spirituality and religion became the central core of human evolution.

Separation took place in every place and in every time. The experience of duality proliferated, closing the dormant human in the golden prison of illusion. Good and evil, the ugly and the beautiful, the good and the bad, but above all the devil and the Holy water became the "programs" that exalt judgment, guilt, and the fear. The presence of the devil became for the Divine-Human a distraction from himself, and the fable of *sin* put the consciousness to sleep.

The disappearance of the Cosmic Bride has divided what is not divisible, has separated the human from his own soul, overshadowing the creative source. Now in the New Time, the awakened human gets rid of the old programs, and returning to the Divine origin, he manifests himself in the Eternal Consciousness of Mary Magdalene.

Myriam, with her return two thousand years later, gives birth to the Female Kristic Seed. The Mary Magdalene who returns is not the feminine energy that replaces the masculine one; she is not the Goddess who takes the place of God; she is not Isis replacing Osiris. She is the kidnapped part that returns to her natural place: there next to her beloved, next to your masculine, in your Heart where she has always and forever lived. There, where man cannot separate what God has united.

The soiled prostitute returns wearing her real clothes. The bride returns in her white dress. Yeshua's beloved returns with her Mastery. Her transparent eyes awaken dormant consciousnesses from the stun of her absence. Her inimitable frequency is recognized in the eyes of those who love her, and the sound of her name vibrates in unison with the primordial one.

During the years many are the stories that have been told about her figure, many are the versions that assert truths about details of her life.

Mary Magdalene is not a story; Mary Magdalene is a call. It is a call that cannot be intellectualized, it is a call that vibrates, it is a beat that pulsates, and it is the love that excites.

In the New Time Myriam returns to teach us the love for life, the love for oneself, what she was already doing back then next to her beloved. She returns to unify in the nuptial room the masculine and feminine aspects. To teach, to Create, to Enjoy and Rejoice: primary goals of earthly existence. Today, in the Time of the New Time, thanks to the return of the Female Kristic Seed, the duality and the separation give way to the Cosmic Union of the androgynous being.

Myriam, Master of the New Energy, returns to spread her Eternal Consciousness. Many will be those who called by its Frequency will hear a familiar reverberation, will enjoy Union and to the religion of Love they will surrender.

Myriam in these pages invites you to feel, to listen, not

to read. She invites you to surrender to your Mastery. She urges you to be *aware* that everything you have experienced in your life so far has been perfect and that nobody but yourself can judge it. In the absence of separation Nothing is ugly; Nothing is beautiful. Nothing is good; Nothing is bad. Everything is Experience. Everything is a creation of You.

Everything is perfect when you let your soul breathe. Live without judging yourself. Love without owning. Breathe without thinking. Laugh for no reason and have fun without waiting any longer.

Happy reading soul companion, Myriam will awaken in You emotions, memories, images. In the New Akashic Rooms, if You so choose, she will invite you to explore yourself and with love she will support you in the experience.

Remember, she does not choose for You. She supports your *choice*. It is You who chooses and creates!

In the name of the Rose, so it is.

2

My Encounter
with Myriam

*M*yriam came at a very painful time of my life—one of the many dark nights of the soul that I went through. I was suffering for a man, or at least I thought that I was suffering for a man, because I thought I fell in love, but in reality I was suffering for my Soul because it is to her that I had not completely given myself.

After returning from a trip to Argentina, I found myself in a pool of blood with a very strong menstrual cycle, high fever, and many tears—not by chance the "cycle," a Sacred symbol that reminded me of my being a Woman. Before leaving for Argentina I had a revealing dream that foretold my encounter with the Sacred Feminine. I dreamt of a woman with dark skin, pregnant in the ninth month, with two large breasts, and on her belly a woman's face that reminded me of that of a shaman.

11

In the dream I looked at myself in a mirror and I recognized myself in that woman.

I left for the land of silver, and I found myself on one of the highest mountains of the world: the Aconcagua, a magic place of very strong emotional intensity. There I met Emilio, the fire-eyed shaman. With him I experimented with particular shamanic rituals that reverberated in me ancient existences. I felt clearly that in those places I had already been. The engraved symbols on the rocks were familiar to me. I knew the way and nothing for me was new. Emilio looked me in the eyes for a long time and with the heart he told me: "Welcome home. This is the valley of the Sacred Feminine. It is Mary who brought you here. Everything else was a means of getting there." At those words I knelt down. I thanked with love that land, and while crumbs of earthy dust flowed through my fingers, I burst into tears.

The shape of the valley was similar to a womb; it really seemed a Universal womb. Emilio spoke with the soul and to the soul, and for my heart it was pure joy. He told me what he felt about me and greeted me before leaving, in a warm embrace that I will never forget. He whispered to me: *"Tu corazón es muy muy grande. No ames a un solo hombre, ama al hombre, ama el mundo, ama la vida. Tú eres el Amor."* (Your heart is very big. Do not love only one man, love the world, love life. You are Love.)

Although I did not fully understand what Emilio had wanted to tell me, everything resonated in the bowels of my belly. But I could not yet imagine what would happen shortly thereafter.

The plane for the return journey was the same, but I was no longer the same. Something had changed in me. I was confused, the rhythm of the heart was altered, and its music was dissonant with my soul who instead rejoiced for the experience that I still did not understand and did not see.

I found myself in a small room with little furniture and four suitcases that contained the essence of a past left behind, with a window from which one could see only silent cypresses. The menstrual cycle abounded, and my body temperature went up, while sweat and chills alternated like in a tribal dance.

The menstruation, symbol of femininity, reminded me of the Divine Woman who was in me. A precious woman for what she was and not because she was pretty and pleasant. A Divine Woman in body and soul simply for what she was in the heart.

In the past I always had a great relationship with my feminine energy. I thought I knew it deeply. I had helped many women to find it and express it. However, the energy of my femininity in that moment that preceded the encounter with Myriam was turning into Sacred Energy, into Divine Energy. I felt clearly inside me an alchemy that flowed through my blood, while deep inside me everything was purified.

The way of the blood reminded me of the purity of the White Rose, the delicacy of the Goddess, and the strength of my womb. The way of the blood reminded me of my Holy Grail, the secret place of alchemical mysteries of my own creation.

That was exactly how she introduced herself. With a Grail full of Hosts before a golden tabernacle, *initiating* me to the Rite of Union. An ancient ritual of times already lived, a vision of known temples, mystery symbols that were no longer mysterious. Everything was clear and natural, where past, present, and future were one: the rediscovered Grail.

After a deep breath I became aware: "Here, this is my Sacred Feminine Energy." An immense heat in the center of my chest like a volcano erupted red lava of rediscovered passion. With a love never known before, she, dressed in white, laid down my naked body in a candid sheet. Baptized and embraced by love.

In that unique and unforgettable moment I experienced the Cosmic Orgasm, and in the heart of my womb I felt the completeness of Myriam and Yeshua finally UNITED.

A fusion that is inexplicable in words. Tears, many tears, while I felt emerging within me the purity of a Woman of other times. A dream, a vision, an astral dream. I cannot explain it to you. What I know is that with a white dress and long auburn hair I saw myself laying down the Holy Grail in a golden tabernacle, aware that from that moment for me it would have been only pure love, Divine Love, and that only a man in love with himself, capable of loving me like Yeshua loved Magdalene, could have *been* Love with me. The Love that it was no longer that of a past woman in the search of love but that of a *Present* woman aware that she herself *is* Love.

I felt an inexplicable peace while the Sacred Union was dancing into my heart in a cosmic marriage. The *Hieros Gamos* had taken place in me.

In her warm fragrant silence, with *Gentle Grace and Sweet Firmness,* she started talking to me: *"I return to unite with him, not to replace him."* This was her first message.

God, how I felt small in front of such beauty, too small in front of so much Light. It was too much for me, or rather, this is what I believed. I understand now that this "too much" that I felt was the mirror of myself. So it was that, knowing of other sisters in the world that loved her so much, I tried with all my strength to involve a Venezuelan friend to come to Italy. However, things got complicated and did not flow naturally . . . I stopped.

I surrendered completely when one night in the company of the full moon and the majesty of the cypresses she talked to me: *"Why do you look for me in the others if I'm here for You?"* Thrills, thrills and tears of deep feeling. An angelic voice accompanied the notes of a harp. Earth was pulsating, the Mother's rhythm was pressing, around me the cypresses and the full moon lightened the darkness of another fear that finally I was letting go. It was then that I completely surrendered to Her, to my Soul and to my Heart that together danced, celebrating my New Life.

"For now keep listening to me without talking about it. Everything will happen as you will be ready. Who will recognize you will love you, who will recognize you will help you. It will not be you talking about it: It will be others looking for you. It will be others calling you. Many will recognize your Presence; many will feel your Frequency, often even your Silence. By looking into your eyes, many people will begin to remember.

Keep spreading what you are with the smile, the simplicity, the Joy, the harmony, the dance, and the SIMPLE language of the heart. Let it all happen and let it all take shape. Start talking about it in a low voice, a thin whisper without too many performances, a light breath, but targeted, precise, and straight to the heart."

Her love like a spring poured inside me, and like a river headed for the sea it began to flow. Her crystal presence with an unmistakable scent sharpened more and more, and the clarity of her messages soon became certainty for me, silencing doubts and fears. As in childbirth I let nine months go by before giving birth to the truth and giving light to her messages. Albeit timidly.

"You will spread the Eternal Consciousness of Me," she told me. *"It is no longer time to persist in knowing my story. It is time to Live me, not to remember me,"* she added.

About her I had read a lot, and many were the stories

that I knew, some of them very different from one another. My human part started to ask her: "But, Myriam, where is the truth? Which one of these stories is true?" With *Gentle Grace*, she answered me:

"See, this is a human question, and it is a question that I will not answer because it is the question of humans' minds that still want to know and understand. Now, in the New Time, it is not time to understand. It is Time to Feel; it is Time to See.

Through You others will feel my Frequency, and with this they will feel their PRESENCE. They will start to feel love for themselves and the deep Connection with their soul. It will happen in a simple, new, and kind way."

Her Frequency resonated in my every cell. I always loved her even when I did not understand the meaning. Since I was a little girl the *fable of the prostitute* did not resonate in me, my being a Woman rebelled, but I did not understand exactly to what. Inside me I felt what I did not understand. Always sure of her INNOCENCE, her way of loving a man shook me, awakening ancient memories in me. Memories that in reality I punctually lived in search of love, without ever feeling loved as I wanted.

As awareness blossomed in the fertile garden of my heart, everything began to be clearer and clearer: the veil of ancient doubts, fears, sins, and useless guilt feelings vanished in front of my Eternal Consciousness. For me it was now clear: no man could have given me that love that I had known and that I always looked for, that love that, in the Eternal Present, is the love of Me.

"Carry on with everything you have Created," she told me. *"Dance, be simple and smile. Keep what you know, but do not attach yourself to it. Intuition is your Teacher. Simplicity will be your strength, and it is with this that, through You, many will surrender joyfully to their own soul. In the Eternal Present everything is simple, everything is a game.*

Spirituality is not a serious matter.

Spirituality is JOY in the MATTER."

It is difficult to understand with the linear mind what I have experienced by encountering her. Maybe you can feel the frequency and this will resonate with you. The *Sound* emits what the eye cannot see. Words cannot explain what is not explainable; words are limited. The love of Myriam, like our Soul, is infinite. Infinite are the experiences that we have lived, life after life, and that have brought us Here.

Here, in the Time of Awakening. Here, now, in the Eternal Consciousness of Mary Magdalene.

In the name of the Rose, so it is.

3

Myriam's Love

*W*hat you have in your hands is not a book.

The written word is a concept, the felt word is a sound, and the *sound* is vibration. Here, it is with this that I urge you to connect. The VIBRATION of these words intones in unison with the frequency of your Divine Self. I am Your thinking heart; I am Your Divine Feminine. When I speak of Divine Feminine, I am not speaking of the woman. I am speaking of the Kristic FREQUENCY imbued in your cells. I am the Kristic Union, and You, through Me, will remember.

Do not ask yourself what. Let it be . . . let it happen.

I only ask you to breathe, yes, a simple breath.

The breath connects you with the heart of the Universe. The breath reminds you of who you are. The breath is the word that becomes a verb. I am not asking you to do it through discipline. I am only asking you to breathe, to simply breathe and to be aware that you are breathing.

Abandon any resistance and ALLOW your soul to breathe into your heart.

The simplicity of the breath is the secret of the soul when it takes shape.

I am Myriam. I would like to introduce myself to You with the name of Myriam and not with that which in the old Consciousness of Me represented the sinner, the prostitute. Mary Magdalene is a sacred and precious name, but in your collective mind it is placed in that part of You that sees me penitent, symbol of sin, the drama and suffering.

No, Master, in the *Eternal Consciousness of Me,* the drama is an ancient memory. Through the Eternal Present the drama transforms itself into Love. The suffering transforms itself into Joy. The sin transforms itself into Freedom.

In the male part of your brain—and with this I am not talking about a man but about that rational part innate in the human—the memory of my suffering image, of my enigmatic image, is preserved, and for many this is mysterious. Even if my story in its various forms has come to light, sometimes it is hard for you to let go of everything that is now in the past. Many still persist in wanting to shed light on my story and on the meticulous details of the places where I lived. Many get lost in my footsteps, on the journey, in search of my relics.

It is no longer time, Master. The journey is what brings you to You. Do not look for my skeleton. With your body, you dress yourself with love.

When you stop looking for me you will have found me.

The obstinacy in distracting himself from his own soul is the way in which the Divine-Human defers the Memory of who he is.

Do not force yourself to understand the details of my story, the dates, the places, the when and how. About this many pages have already been written, and many of these you have already read. Many have excited you; others have intrigued you. Precious and exhaustive writings by which the writer, with his heart, sought himself through me. Precious writings by which he sought lost love through me. Loving writings by which he sought the Spirit through the union of me and Yeshua. Each story that you have read has left you with something. If there was a story that resonated in you, let it be; do not strive to find more in the long-gone past.

The New Time is NOW. The New Time is PRESENCE.

Many of the writings will serve the dormant humans who still rest in oblivion of human life.

Let it be. Let each person have his or her own journey.

Be a lighthouse not a lantern.

To You who reads, what do you still need to look for? What and who are you looking for? Is it really me who you are looking for? Or through Me you are looking for Yourself? If you are listening to the sounds of these words, You are no longer one of the dormants, you are among those who know, among those who have for years and years traveled inside and outside themselves looking for the Spirit in every place and in every teacher, just as my beloved did. He too in his journey, which began as a teenager, discovered that the Divine Spark he had always looked for dwelt in the womb of the Mother Goddess imbued with his own Being.

What happened to me under that almond tree in the moment Yeshua looked at me in the soul is perhaps what is happening to You as you now allow Your soul to look you into your eyes.

Now I ask you: what would change in your life if you knew for sure that with my beloved, besides having loved each other deeply, we joined in marriage? What would change in You if you were sure that Sarah was in my womb? And that maybe Yeshua continued to unite with my soul and with my body even after death?

What would change in your life knowing that it is true that it was Joseph of Arimathea who accompanied me to the places in the south of France to escape from those who wanted my death? What would change in You if you discovered for sure that the *fleur-de-lis* is really the expression of the royal line of children I had? What would change in You knowing that under the Tower of Magdala a treasure is hidden?

What would change in your life?

You would know more about my Story, but what about the Story of your soul, what do you know?

Master, in the New Time, it is not what happened to me

that will change Your life but what you discover of You that will Transform Yours.

When you stop looking for me, you will have found me.

You will discover that I have always been inside You and so the truth will come out effortlessly. The Divine truth that you will see outside You will be the mirror of Your newfound truth about who You Are.

Many are those who, since I have left Myriam's body, in the places where my perfume of myrrh is still felt today, fascinated by my story, looked for me in every place, in every papyrus, and in every corner where it is said that I have lived. Many are those who still persist in wanting to "understand" my story. Many are those who through my Story have fed their own Power.

Master, it is not my story that must be understood, but the Frequency that I AM that must be embodied. This is what helps you *remember* Your Story. This is what helps you remember who you Are. In the places where I lived, you can now enjoy the Beauty of You. You can enjoy the rediscovered Grail, and with it you can celebrate the *promise* fulfilled, yes, that promise made then, that first time. Remember?

The Frequency that I AM is what, life after life, inhabited the bodies of many Women and Men that you know well and of which I will tell you later. Now it is Time to live me, not to look for me. It is Time to live me, not to remember me. If you keep looking for Me, forgetting Yourself, my writings will never be found. It is part of the game of the

Creation. It is part of the initial PROMISE: while you seek the Union outside Yourself, the Treasure will remain hidden.

Now you are asking yourself: "Myriam, how can I live you?"

You can live me by living You. I am the energy of Transformation that is in You when you let yourself go to change. I am the Kristic Frequency instilled in your DNA. I am the vibration of the UNION that in your thinking heart Creates the integration of Your own life.

In recent times there is much talk about the Goddess and her return. I want you to understand that the Goddess is not the woman as a female form but the *creative being* present in each Divine-Human. The creative being is not male nor female. It is the androgynous being that has always housed Your soul. It is the cosmic womb in which Your creations grow. It is your creative solution that frees the prison of mass consciousness thoughts. The Goddess is your own Life! I am You; I am that part of You forgotten and dormant over the centuries by the occult power. I am the Energy of balance, the frequency of Union, the vibration of Transformation.

Through the Ray of me that writes I come to You to spread my Eternal Consciousness. With Gentle Grace and Sweet Firmness, I come to You in the New Time, I come to You in the Time of the Mother, in the Time of Change, in the Time of Transformation. I come to You to remind you who you Are, not who I Am.

"I return to unite with him, not to replace him." This is the first message I conveyed to the Ray, thanks to which You now read me. I am not coming to You to replace God; I am not coming to You to replace Yeshua or any other divinity.

Master, I am the Energy of Union. I am the frequency of love. Love, the love for yourself, love, what I and Yeshua have shared. God how much I loved him. God how much he loved me.

The Union, this is the perfume of the Eternal consciousness.

My invitation is not to exalt the woman but to invite the woman to UNITE with herself. The exaltation of the woman alone leads the man to close himself in his masculine with his hidden insecurity. The man, and therefore the masculine aspect that is in You, needs to let go to his feminine aspect. Whether you are a man or a woman, ALLOW your Divine Masculine that is in You to let go to Your Sacred Feminine. Yes, I know that now you are asking yourself: "But how can I do this?"

By listening to You. By welcoming You. By respecting You. By forgiving You. By understanding You.

By feeling compassion for Yourself.

By forgiving You for castrating yourself for centuries and centuries of the most creative part of your being. You who are woman in a physical sense: the more you unite with yourself the more you will accompany the man to unite with the woman who is inside him. By seeing you

UNITED he will feel complete, and in You he will no longer seek the unique love of a mother, nor the nostalgia of the lost bride, nor the challenge of a rival. By letting go of the fear of not being loved, he will see you like a mirror of his Beauty. With Sweet Firmness, he will let himself go into the arms of her feminine being, and only then in pure love he will feel FREE.

There is not a superior or inferior being between a woman and a man. There is no weakness and strength. This is the dichotomy of the old time. This is the dichotomy of religious power. There is the awakening and the return to the origin of the Divine-Human. As it happened to me and Yeshua, men and women will be Masters of Love and the others will feel it in their frequency. The frequency of the DNA that awakens will be the new music of the Universe that will accompany the Divine-Human to create his New Life.

Put down your sword. In the New Time there are no more Romans, no Pilates, no stakes, no crusades. Nobody, except yourselves, can separate you from what is not separable, and your life will not be the end of an old story but the beginning of a long love story.

Breathe . . . let it be. Breathe . . . let it happen.

A new love story between You and your soul. She—who since your first incarnation, in the becoming of her journey, life after life—has always loved you and brought you here. Here, in the Awareness of your awakening, the same

Awareness that my beloved lived in his mystical journey in search of himself. That mysterious journey of which the yellowed pages of doctrines have revealed with occult silence. He too for almost twenty years searched in the mystery of every place, in the pain, in the silence and in the solitude, until he got inside himself. There he stopped, and it is there that in the eyes of Spirit he recognized himself.

What Yeshua lived in his journey is the mirror of what You also lived to get here. Here where you are today. Here, in the Time of Awakening. Here, in the Time of Creation. Here, in that chair while you read me. Here, in your safe place where you hear my voice. Here, in Your heart where You feel at home.

Many of you have fallen in love with Mary Magdalene, forgetting her ancient frequency. The ancient frequency of the origin. I came from far away, and I continued to infuse myself into the body of Women and Men that have made history. Just like then, my beloved told me, many are the times that I have returned. Clare, Francis's love, maybe it reminds you of something? Now do not look for dates, books, and different notes closed in your library.

Now, in this instant, stop, breathe, breathe and remember.

I do not teach you anything, I just put you in a position to remember.

Joan, Joan of Arc. Does it tell you anything? Vittoria, Vittoria Colonna loved by the great Master. Does it tell you anything? Have you ever asked yourself why the great Master changed his work by replacing my face with the one he loved spiritually? And why did the Master leave his body looking at me until his last breath? Breathe, silence your mind, breathe, do not try to understand, remember, maybe you were there too in these lives of mine and that is why you have always looked for me. Bodies that have hosted My Frequency, just as Yours has been from life to life hosted by the different experiences that have served you to get here. Here, in the Time of Now where the helices of your DNA unwind, returning to the origin.

My journey ends in the Time of the MOTHER through the experience of this Ray that like a sun warms the dormant heart of the Divine-Human and with the name of the Rose announces itself.

The journey of my soul is Your own journey, the one you have also done to get to discover Your Divine Spark. It is the journey that brought you to know your soul, that soul mate who has never left you from that first instant of the initial PROMISE. That soul mate you have always looked for outside You.

I know how much you have suffered. I know how many times you thought you could not make it, how many times you felt *home*sick, how many times you have looked for me, how many times you have believed in a SIN that you have never committed, how many times you felt alone, and how many times in your solitude you have believed yourself insane. Master, you were in the labyrinth in the search of your Soul. You lost yourself to find yourself right now, now, in the center of your ROSE.

I invite you to Enjoy your perfume. I invite you to Enjoy Yourself. Stop looking for my Story. Enjoy Yours. Stop trying to understand who I Was and find out who You Are. Only then you will have truly found me, and finally you will have found the whole truth. Only then you will feel me in every breath and you will no longer need to know or seek. You will live me, leaving me that place that has always been mine. Your Sacred Feminine returns to its place, there, where by Divine right it is natural to be.

Breathe dancing soul, dance the life, live your body, cancel any separation and through my Frequency unite your Masculine and your Feminine into One. You and your infinite aspects are One. You, complete with You, and the others, complete with themselves, are One. No one can be with another if he lacks himself.

Yes, soul companion, no one can be with another if he lacks himself.

I was Yeshua's beloved, and this can no longer be concealed. With my beloved we loved each other in the Body, in the Mind, and in the Spirit. With Yeshua we shared pure love, Sacred love, and we United to Cosmic love. Under the shadow of an almond tree, he recognized my gaze; in his voice, I recognized the sound of the origin. The almond tree, the sacred tree with an atavistic meaning—the almond, amygdala, the Tower—he told me: *"You will be the Shepherdess of*

the Tower," the tower that connects Earth to the Sky, the Sacred Zed that in the Time of Awakening, silent and attentive, observes and waits a little longer.

The love between me and Yeshua was pure love: his passion warmed my soul, his gaze read into my heart, his hands wrapped my body.

Together with Yeshua, we taught to love oneself first. The occult power of the church was afraid of the Cosmic Union and, in every way, tried to separate you from Your Feminine part, making you forget who you Are. It wrote and told fables steeped in drama, fear, SIN, and suffering that distract you from Yourself. When I speak of truth, I do not just mean what has not been said and what has been withheld. The truth is the one in which the Divine-Human reveals himself in his true nature and finally understands who HE IS. He finally understands that he himself is the Creator of his own life. Finding out what in the womb of Earth he came to experiment, this is the truth. Finding out who you Are and, without any more burdens of the past, surrender to Your Mastery, this is the truth.

You are an ANGEL. You are an ANGEL dressed as a Human. This is the truth.

Now based on Your New Awareness I ask you: knowing that Yeshua had one, two, three, or more brothers, or that Mary did not die a virgin, or many other questions that you have always asked yourself, is it still that important to You?

Persisting in looking for me outside of Yourself and continuing to ask questions about me, don't you think it would imitate the same experience that you lived back then, when you were perhaps a Cathar or a Templar? Masters, it is no longer time to fight, it is no longer time to take sides, it is no longer time to separate from the pleasure like you did then. The Spirit in the Matter is to Love yourself. The light body merges into the physical body and in unison, in the name of the Mother, raises the sword in honor of the rediscovered soul. This is the Heavenly Jerusalem.

I know that maybe some of you are crying right now, others are smiling, and still others are angry. Breathe, any emotion that advances, breathe, let it happen. Whatever is your experience or whoever You have been, know that today you no longer need to know, nor can you remain ATTACHED to a previous life.

Forgive Yourself, you are not at fault.

Forgive Yourself, you are not at fault.

Accusing yourself no longer serves you. Don't you think that it was already a high price to pay on the part of your soul, that life after life, existence after existence, has returned each time to evolve? It was an experience. An experience that together with the companion souls of your Spiritual Family you had chosen before descending. There was a deep agreement among you. Do you remember? You needed it to get here in the Time of Awakening, and it All made sense. In the New Time you have nothing left, neither to understand nor to accuse yourself. You only have to LIVE.

NOW, thanks to the New Frequency, you are learning to let go of everything you no longer need. In the New Time you do not need shoes to walk; you need wings to fly. In the New Time everything becomes light because there is no past to suffer for, but there is a Present with which to Create.

Master, stop fighting. Hang the sword on the nail, remove the helmet, get off your horse, and gallop through life for the sole pleasure of being FREE.

Listen to the voice of your Consciousness: "You Are the Creator of Your Life. You Are What You Are."

I love you, soul companion, I love You deeply . . .

In the name of the Rose, so it is.

4

An Aspect
Is Not the Story

*N*ow, before continuing to listen to these pages, I want to tell you the story of an aspect of Mary Magdalene, but know that an aspect is not the story. Just like an Aspect of You, is not You.

When I was born, my mother did not desire me and my father wanted a boy.

Now, if you are crying as you read this, it is because this may have happened to You.

Breathe, breathe, do not do anything, breathe, soul companion. Breathe deeply and allow the new You to create her space.

Not being desired, I carried the emptiness of love with me already from the dawn of the day of my birth, when silence welcomed my first cry. As I grew up, the emptiness of love became a chasm, and I begged outside for crumbs of love as nourishment.

I did not know what love was and did not understand from where it could be drawn. I continued to feel drained by looks that longed for my fresh and adolescent body. Having no energy and not knowing how to do it, I began to painfully satiate myself with those hands playing with my scented woman's body. Not knowing the source from which I needed to feed myself, I began to feed myself with attention, albeit painful and insatiable.

I was desired for my beauty and womanliness, but this substitute for love began to stun me.

Breathe, soul companion, be it tears, anger, or whatever feeling comes up now in this instant . . . Breathe, breathe, and let it flow, do nothing . . . Whether You are a man or a woman, Breathe, breathe deeply. This kind of violence may seem strange to you, but it also happened to You man. To You man, who in every woman has sought me out, to You who has touched Your Heart with continuous requests for recognition that have been made to you. To You man who in seeking motherly love in every woman have forgotten Your Soul.

The emptiness in me grew and the external nourishment became more and more insipid. Many times I have thought that only death could have really nourished me. I was wrong: death is not the end, death is a pause. I reached a point where I wished to die with all my strength, but I did not yet know that soon after that, the male I had feared so much would be ready to love me unconditionally.

The gaunt face could not obscure the innocence of my eyes and the beauty of who I really was. Leaves of trees danced to the music of the wind, while *He,* looking into my eyes, recognized me. I was too blind to go further, and first I saw only the man in him. Having the NEED to feed myself, I was quick to offer myself. I was amazed and baffled when my ears heard the music of these words:

"Do not worry. I will give you what you need, but you will not have to give me anything in return."

Inside me Earth trembled, the sea flooded every cell of mine, the fire burned in my heart that did not understand, and in the air a scent of white rose suffused my sense of smell.

"What?" I asked him. "Would you be truly willing to give me love without asking for anything in return?"

He looked into my eyes for a long time. A look that I had never seen before. It was God who looked at me for the first time; indeed, it was I who saw him for the first time.

Some of the men who accompanied him were sometimes attracted by my beauty, but he did not allow anyone to get close to me, to seek the love I am, which was blossoming from the muck of pain.

He often spoke to me just looking at me. Only through the gaze, without ever touching each other, we made love. He taught me to take care of Me, to love Me, to respect Me, telling me that no one could do it for me. I began to feed on Me, and gradually that emptiness of love was filled in with Crystal Water baptizing me with pure love.

It was thus that I awakened in me the memory of Isis, of the Essene Master I was and of the GREAT MOTHER at the origin of the *sound*. Life after life, I went back to my memories, when the Feminine Creative Energy blew into the clay and gave shape to the mirror image of God. Yeshua recognized me and loved me for who I was. Full of love and Divine awareness, I began to approach him to share the love I was and not the love I was looking for.

It was then that full of love for me our bodies united, merging into the Sacred Creative Energy. We were both a mirror of love for each other, and as the ancestral energy flowed through our naked bodies canceling the separation, the awakening of the androgynous being sealed our Love. Two in one, one in two, as in a dance, everything flowed in candid purity and burning Passion without sin.

Breathe soul companion, breathe . . . breathe and remember.

Now, while you are reading, I feel in You a strange nostalgia of love, an aspect of You that makes you think: "How nice to find unconditional love that loves you just as you are."

The story that I told you must be decoded, and it is even deeper than it appears. Go inside, breathe and go forward into the bowels of your belly, there, in that point where you will meet Yourself.

Yeshua is the masculine aspect that is in You. He is the Male Kristic Seed. He is the masculine aspect of You that loves you for what You Are. He is the aspect of You that Loves to act without re-acting. Whether You are a man or a woman, it is the DIVINE masculine aspect that is in You that, tired of being pointed out, judged, and demanded, surrenders to love.

Now, this story can also be a metaphor, it does not matter. Let it instill within You what You need. Let what is true for You reverberate in You.

Yeshua and I in the Eternal Present, we are FREQUENCY, not an image, not a memory, not a statue to idolize. We are the frequency of the Inner Union that returns in the Time of Awakening to experience the Completeness.

With Yeshua we UNITED in the Mind, in the Spirit, and also in the Body only when our fullness of love was completely filled with our Divinity. It has never happened before. Two Masters are Masters when together they share love, not when they seek love.

Making love with the other without Loving yourself is not making love. It is seeking Love.

If you want you can give it other names; it does not matter. History has written many names and stories. Do not give too much importance to the words: feel the frequency, feel its vibration, feel the sound. It is the one that vibrates and from which everything Originates.

Close your eyes for a moment, allow Your silence to speak. Breathe and hear Your sound. Empty the Chalice and fill it with the Breath of You.

As you can see this is not a book. It is a sound; it is a sound that awakens You. It is a call from Your soul. It is a chorus of a song that reminds You of the music that you already know.

Do not follow your thoughts. Let your feelings guide You.

Trust Yourself, let it be, let it happen. Breathe.

Many have written many stories about my life, my childhood, my family: where I lived, where I ran away, if I really had a daughter or if this daughter was never born. If I was married to Yeshua. If I had other children even after Yeshua's death. What you just heard could be another story. Now I know that your linear mind is asking: "But then where is the truth? Which one of the many stories is the true one?" Here, this is the first question that the Ray, thanks to whom you read me, asked me, when I awakened my Frequency in Her. It is the question of the collective mind that still seeks to know, to understand, and to connect.

The Eternal Consciousness of Mary Magdalene is the "feeling" of the New Time, and therefore it is to your feeling that I leave the answer.

Master, everything that is old you no longer need to know. Wanting to know is the old You, and this belongs to that limited part of You, to that part of You that seeks confirmations, securities, proofs, and certainties.

You are unlimited; the human limit is an illusion.

Let Yourself go and listen to You, love You, welcome You without judging You. This is Respect. This is Love for You.

Express Your sweetness without fear of being judged, express Your sensitivity, cry if you want to cry, and laugh if you want to laugh. You are a set of aspects, and an aspect is not the story. You are an androgynous being, and the UNION is within You. Not outside You, not in a woman, not in a man. Inside, inside You, in the altar of Your heart.

This is the Time of Transformation of all the ancient patterns. The burdens you have taken on over the centuries vanish in the water of the New Time. A Crystal Water that in the name of the MOTHER baptizes You in the river of the New Jerusalem.

I love You, and I welcome You, soul companion . . .

In the name of the Rose, so it is.

5

New Akashic Rooms

*R*egister, Memory, Library, Chronicle. These are some of the names with which the AKASHA has been defined in the becoming of different eras.

The word *akasha* is a Sanskrit sound. A melodic sound that changes frequency through the New Time. Each Divine-Human in his different existences has experienced a myriad of experiences, and these, from life to life, have echoed in the infinite space leaving traces of memories.

In the Eternal Consciousness of Mary Magdalene the Akasha is Transformed.

The Sound of Remembering becomes the sound of Presence.

The Divine-Human, awakened from oblivion, transforms the frequency of his earthly abode, and coming out of the linear mind, he begins to wander in those energetic rooms once considered only elite places where, during the hibernation of humanity, only a few could access. Now, it is no longer time.

Now, the human Creator accesses his CENTER becoming the channel that channels his own Consciousness.

In the New Time the Divine-Human, aware of his multidimensionality and of his infinite *aspects,* wanders in the infinite worlds, and through his ability to get out of the linear mind, he visits the experiences of his previous lives without taking them on anymore. He visits them, explores them, observes them, honors them, contacts them, and integrates them with self-awareness. He is aware that the energy of those previous lives is his because he lived through those experiences. He takes on a drop of the essence of what he needs as a potential awakening and allows the death of what is no longer useful for his evolution. He knows that the past is not himself, but only the experience of what he lived in that moment.

In the New Time, memory is not a recollection. In the present, Consciousness is PRESENCE.

Mary Magdalene is not a memory.

Mary Magdalene is a Presence.

Mary Magdalene is the frequency that AWAKENS.

Mary Magdalene is the frequency of the origin.

Archive, Memory, Chronicle become obsolete sounds that reveal a linear list. A database of information written in now illegible faded ink on yellowed paper. In the New Energy, there are no linear paths toward which to head; there are no peaks to aspire to for the unbridled desire to arrive at a destination. The summit to be reached is not the top of the mountain to which every master aspired in the past. The summit of the mountain in the Time of Now is the Center. The Center that in every place and in every time remains the Center of oneself.

The frequency of Earth in the Creator's Time is Circular, not linear.

In the New Time, there is no past coming back; there is a Present to Live.

There is no karma to atone; there is a Present to Enjoy.

There is no past to cling to.

There is a Present in which to BREAK FREE.

Let go of excuses related to memories of previous lives, which cause you to postpone taking responsibility for your life. These excuses lose strength when confronted with the evidence of the human need for change, with the human who acquires more and more awareness of his Divine being, with the human who takes responsibility for his own life and who, without excuses, stops being distracted.

The Akasha of the New Time is a hymn to the change.

It is a transition from Human to Divine, from Dormant to Creator.

If in the past you have had experiences in which you have felt guilt, fear, doubt, and uncertainty, and you have seen, explored, and integrated these feelings, it is no longer useful for you to remain attached to those old experiences and perceptions. When you know it but you keep doing it, you stay in the old hospital of victimhood. You are only pro-crastinating, avoiding the choice to take on the responsibility for being the Creator of your own life. What will happen is that you will remain in this energy addiction and attract to you someone who will try to heal you, convincing you that ONLY his remedy is the right one for you.

Learn the law of discernment and observe. Does the other do it for you or for himself?

Knowledge, without self-awareness, is nothing.

Soul companion, it is only within YOU that you will find the Energy with which to nourish and heal yourself.

Healing yourself means learning to be WHOLE. Whole and complete with every part of YOU.

The energy of the Eternal Consciousness of Mary Magdalene is INTEGRAL. With Sweet Firmness she brings you to YOU, not to HER.

Breathe . . . breathe deeply. Breathe . . .

The *Circular Rooms* to which Myriam will invite you to enter are infinite SPACES where you can explore Yourself, if you want to.

Circular Rooms in which to experiment new experiences, acquire new awarenesses, see the infinite aspects, and allow potentials to manifest.

The Mastery of the Creator is only through the Awareness that manifests. Know that there are no other ways.

Breathe, breathe, soul companion, breathe deeply and feel whether really deep inside you there is the desire to explore the *Circular Rooms* where the frequency that speaks to you invites you to enter.

Ask your Consciousness. SHE knows.

The responsibility whether to enter it or not will be Yours and nobody else's. In the New Time, you cannot blame anyone. In the New Time, Time is Yours, and only You will know what to do with it.

Breathe, breathe deeply. Let go of all expectations. If you really have to expect something, expect the UNIMAGINABLE. The story is not how it was told to you. The story must be created.

In the name of the Rose, so it is.

6

The Mother

*W*ith Gentle Grace to you I address . . .

To You, Woman. To you, Mother. To YOU, MOTHER of new children. To You, Mother of new smiles. To You, Mother of new looks. To You, who feel the gasp of the Joy of life in the womb. To YOU, who give birth and give birth to You. To You, BRIDGE of earthly life.

Divine Mother the Time has changed!

During the journey that led the Divine-Human to awaken, the soul that chose you as a Mother, in Your WATER, took charge of your emotions, and your conscience became heavy with ancient burdens. Circular generations have perpetuated themselves in the cycle of Human existence. A cycle that has now exploded. A cycle that has now expanded. A cycle that has now ended. Thanks to the Eternal Consciousness, Earth today breathes and vibrates with a new frequency. Let it be. Let it happen. Do nothing. Even when fear knocks, do nothing. Fear is the absence of love for Yourself. Live it without judging yourself, welcome it without understanding it, and nourish it with the love of You by Transforming it.

The New Children cross the bridge with no more drama.

The New Children know who they are.

The New Children are here to help you. They are here for the final cleansing of the planet. Many of them will do it by dancing, painting, singing, but above all Rejoicing. Many of them will tell you about new discoveries useful for the healing of Mother Earth. They will reveal to you secrets in front of which you can only surrender and learn. You will have in front of You a small body with a Great Soul.

They are the ones who, with simplicity and naturalness, will tell you what happens beyond the veil and with love will help you to understand that death is only an illusion. The Masters of the new womb will bring archaic messages from ancient times. Through the Universal placenta they will help you to let go of the last dross. They will come to talk to you about the time that has changed, and like my Beloved, already as children they will speak to the crowd. By listening to them you will forget their age because they are ageless. The new souls will bring the feminine energy to the planet. I am not saying that many girls will be born. I am saying that many souls will be born with a strong feminine energy, that creative force inherent in every Divine-Human. That force that reminds You of Your androgynous being. That force that reminds You of the power of Creation.

The New Sons will no longer be afraid to express their feminine energy. They will no longer need to prove their strength with false Power. They will no longer have nostalgia for the womb. They will create from the heart and with the heart they will give birth to new frequencies.

The Masters Return. Let it Be. Let it Happen.

Welcome them, let them do it. Welcome them, let them guide you.

Time has changed. It is not the old that dictates; it is the New that INVITES.

Let it Be. Let it happen.

Mother of life, Honor your Creations. Every Creation that IS BORN of You is a Creature, and every Creature is the fruit of your heart, of Your heart destined to give birth to love.

I welcome you in my Universal womb, and I love You deeply.

You are Love, and in love You are the way.

New discoveries await you, if the New attracts you continue exploring this Experience. If the old calls You back or still distracts You, maybe it is better that You take some time to Breathe.

Breathe . . . breathe deeply.

Do you hear a sound?

Do you feel a New Frequency?

It is You!

Originally, you were SOUND, and to experience love, in the silence of the breath You took shape.

IN THE AKASHIC ROOMS

The room that we see in front of our eyes is circular, no corners, no stairs, no corridors, an infinite space where everything breathes within a spiral.

Before entering, we are asked if we really want to open up to the New. A gift is also made to us. It is a spherical Crystal. Inside it is hollowed out. It seems to have the appearance of a place not yet discovered; it is as if it were meant to be a prophetic clue. Looking at it better, our attention is captured by an underlying code: it is the number three, repeated three times. Without too much understanding, we are grateful in the heart for the gift received.

"The frequency of this Crystal is the same that you will find inside the Circular Rooms, from this you will be able to Remember. From this you will be able to Create. The choice will be Yours!"

Like children eager to play, the desire to go forward grows, dismantling doubts and fears. The choice of whether to open up to the New or to stay in the old will be the key to the experience we are going to have.

Before going forward we are asked to put down the heavy karmic bags:

"In the New Energy you do not need them. In the New

Energy there is not a past that holds back; there is a PRESENT that welcomes."

The invitation to enter the room of the Present excites us. We soon understand that the energy of the New is in abundance everywhere. Like clay, the human sculptor can model it and give it the shape that he has *chosen* to Create.

The spiral light begins to transform; waves of fluorescent colors sway sensually. The frequency is very high, lightweight in the Timeless Space. The *Circular Room* lights up with GOLD. Immersed in the abundance of love, the Golden Ray appears in its beauty.

Here she is . . .

With Gentle Grace and Sweet Firmness, Myriam looks into the eyes of our soul, smiles at us, and supports our Choice, invites us to enter. Waiting for us is HER, the Mother, the Great Mother, the Mother of all MOTHERS, the womb guardian of the Male Kristic Seed. The Heavenly MOTHER. The Master Mother who for the collective imagination only represented the archetype of the poor and suffering Mother.

You would not think so, as a radiant smile greets us.

The always fresh face of a timeless Woman seems to have something New to tell us. Her Presence is so reassuring that the only thing we want is to hear what she has to say and see what she has to show to us.

"I know you expected to find me in tears under the cross or in the cold in an icy cave, but as you can see, this is not the

case. I also know that many of the things I will tell you at the beginning may upset you, but if you remain in the frequency of that Crystal that was given to you before moving on, everything I will tell you will be able to awaken healthy memories in you.

As happened to my beloved Magdalene, I too have lived in the shadows for centuries. Except for the tears under the cross and the pangs of childbirth in the cold of a cave, my story as a Woman has only been talked about through the Silence."

"How in the shadows?" Joy states in amazement.

"You have been worshipped on all altars. Loved by religion. Adored by the Priests and by the many Popes who have made history. What do you mean by shadow?" he adds.

"I was loved as the Madonna, Virgin of Sorrow. But of Mary the Woman, what is known? Of me, Essene Master, what is known? Of my life, what is known? Nothing!

What is the message that was transmitted through me in the pages yellowed by the occult? What is the information that through my figure has imbued the minds of Divine-Human with drama and suffering? Besides the time of birth and death of my beloved son, what is known, what is said about Me in the traditional scriptures?

Nothing, only drama.

Together with my beloved Magdalene, we have been stamped from history with roles that do not belong to us. The Mother as Madonna. The Magdalene as a prostitute.

Myriam and I loved each other deeply as companions, as

Masters, and as Women aware of their Mastery and of the Ancient Secrets.

Originally, the Mother Goddess gave birth to Earth. To remember her fertile color, she dyed my face dark. Thus it was that I was brought to twenty-two points that connect Earth to the infinite worlds. In the initial project each point was to be a passage from the astral to the physical world. The Sacred Bridge, the Passage from Knowledge to the Experience of the I Am. From the believer to the creator.

The Mother's Creative Cup had to be forgotten, hidden, dressed, concealed, renamed, bleached, and continuously moved from one place to another to confuse, to distract, to forget what is not forgettable.

The Great Mother thus infused herself in the womb of every Mother, life after life, ray after ray, woman after woman. Compared to Magdalene, accused of being the seductive human provocation, after years of forced Silence, I have been recognized as the Divine female figure by those who avail themselves of the Kristic truth.

A Woman representing pain would not have been a danger. A Virgin Woman would not have been a sin. A Woman to be idolized would have obscured the awareness of one's own ability to Create. Everything was much simpler. Everything could be controlled by the masculine energy. When I speak of masculine, I am not speaking of a man in a physical sense. I am talking about that masculine energy of the occult power that over the centuries, to maintain its advantage, has taken over.

By coloring my story through the Virginity of my fertile womb, the Sacred Energy, with which humans unite in physical love and thanks to which the MOTHER gives birth to the Life itself, has been polluted. False information has been transmitted that the Feminine Divinity is Sacred only if Virgin and that the expression of the Sacred Sexual Energy is Sin and that this sin is the origin of evil. This is the program that shaped the Consciousness of guilt and shame. This same consciousness became the prison in which the Divine-Human found himself serving punishments for acts never committed. The collective consciousness injected with SIN thus became a cudgel with which to beat one's chest, each time reinforcing the awareness of a sinful ghost. Shame and guilt, hand in hand, collaborated in the most daring separation of the centuries: Yourself from Your SOUL.

Master, I would like to remind you that the only sin that You can commit is to not Love yourself. Using Your Creative Energy without loving yourself, this is sin. Not understanding who you Are, this is a shame. The Creating energy cannot be polluted with the love of You. It can darken with the lack of love for You.

Yes, it is from the MOTHER that these words come to You.

A MOTHER who frees You from the guilt over a wrongdoing you never committed.

A MOTHER who baptizes You with the water of her womb.

A MOTHER who invites You to see the Mother who is within You.

Regardless of whether You are a man or a woman, every time you Create Your life, You are a MOTHER.

Sin, drama, sacrifice, these are seeds that made harmful beliefs germinate in human minds, stunning the far-sighted vision of the human.

In every statue, in every procession, they depicted me in tears in search of my dead son. As with my beloved Myriam, the icons that have always depicted us cry stories of drama. Please, stop painting tears. Magdalena's beloved is alive! My beloved SON is ALIVE! Because that son, that daughter is You. It is You who awakens! You who discover to be God-Goddess who CREATES. You who awaken the Seed of Creation in your DNA.

Now I will tell you a story of Yeshua a little different from that of your collective consciousness. You will be Free to believe it or not, my invitation is: Breathe, go into the heart and listen.

Breathe deeply into your belly and feel deep within Yourself if there is something that resonates with you.

Since childhood he loved being called by his real name: Yeshua. He was just a young boy when, meeting the gaze of his soul he began his spiritual quest. Just like You, he wanted to become a teacher of the Spirit, so it was that he chose a school, for him it was the Essene one. It was too rigid for his strongly rebellious and passionate nature. He loved his body and his human part and never deprived himself of the experience that he could experiment through it. He loved to laugh, cry, and enjoy the Temple of his soul. This put him very much in contrast with the rigid doctrine that he had imposed on himself through the school to which he belonged. He did not like to turn water into wine or even walk on water. He loved to walk on Earth, and many are the steps he took in his journey in search of himself.

'What?' someone might think, 'but he was the son of God. Why would he have to look for what he already was?'

And YOU. Why do you keep looking for what you already are?

His journey is the same that You also made to get here, here in the Time of Creation.

Little more than a little boy, Yeshua lived many dark nights of the soul that brought him against what he had learned in his Essene school. Just as You did that time you left that school, he too chose to abandon it, and perhaps just like it happened to You, he too felt abandoned and lost. He was about eighteen years old when among sand grains of the desert he saw all aspects of himself mingle with the notes of the music of the wind, there, in that first place where he had chosen to listen to his Spirit. The talkative silence of that place began to talk to him about something else and, in his journey outside and inside him, pushed him BEYOND.

He began to learn more about the Temple that housed his soul. He experienced the knowledge of the energy movement and surrendered to it eager to explore himself. Just like You, he was attracted by the lands to the East, and even later, he

let himself be caressed by the soft curves of other places, where he reliably never found what he was looking for. Just like You in all those times when you gave up your power to that guru, to that discipline, or perhaps to that illusory experience, he too sought outside himself what he had inside. He spent a lot of time in his beloved pyramids that he knew so well from previous experiences, and there he learned a lot. Like You, he met many Masters, and with many of them shared discoveries that were very different from what he had always believed up to then. He emptied the cup of his knowledge and with great humility began to fill with New Knowledge, which gradually brought him deeper and deeper into himself. With a smile on his lips, he learned to breathe, fully understanding how the Breath was the true Master.

As his journey unfolded, he too learned that God was not in the clouds to judge the good and the bad and that this separation was far from God's love. He learned that there was no God who, depending on the mood in which he woke up, rewarded or punished. He learned that God was not in the places where he had always sought him, but that the journey had been the means to get to find him within Himself, just like it happened to You.

He experienced self-love, self-compassion, and self-acceptance, and looking at himself in the transparency of a river dear to him, he recognized his Spirit.

He clearly understood that the journey of life was about himself and that the school could never be a community.

His own life, his own journey was the school. He under-stood that he could never teach what he knew, but he could transmit to others what he WAS. Only his Essentiality could be the MATER through which to spread the purpose of his existence on Earth.

Maybe this also happened to You . . .

Breathe, soul companion, breathe and listen . . .

Yeshua, after his long journey that lasted almost twenty years, felt the desire to return to the places where he was born. This too has probably happened to some of you who are listening. He followed his heart without rules and thus chose to return to his land to teach how to SEEK God within oneself, to spread the awareness that only unconditional love for oneself was the SECRET.

On his arrival he was not welcomed with open arms by everyone; many criticized him. This also happened to You, right? Yes, it happened all those times that you have tried to bring Your New Awareness to others, especially your loved ones, and they criticized you because you were no longer the same, and you were no longer in that familiar Consciousness within which you had identified for years.

Those who felt within themselves the reverberation of the Spirit wishing to express himself followed him. Aware of being himself God, with the Passion and the charisma of his soul, Yeshua began to transmit the experience of his journey.

He met Myriam, and he fell madly in love with her

Innocent gaze. It was Pure love, a Great sensual, passionate, simple, and elegant love story.

When Yeshua together with his beloved began to teach love, acceptance, and compassion toward oneself, many were those who began to follow him, but many saw in him a Master to idolize.

Yeshua did not like to be worshipped. He wanted to see in the eyes and smiles of those who loved him the awareness of the newfound Divinity; this was what gave him a Great Joy. He soon realized that there were many who put TRUST in him and not in themselves. He felt in the depths of his gut that humanity was not ready to rejoice in his own Mastery. He felt that it would take another two millennia before anything could happen and that this would happen through the Feminine Energy, through the energy and the FREQUENCY of his Beloved Myriam.

The Collective Consciousness was not yet ready to recognize God within itself. Yeshua did not want people to make him GOD, but he deeply desired that every Divine-Human recognize the GOD within himself, not in a doctrine, not in a dogma, not in a discipline, not in a Master, but in the inner God-Goddess, as a fragment and particle of the same Divine substance.

His beloved kept the Royal Blood in her GRAIL, in her womb she preserved the fruit of their love. Yes, the sweet and passionate Myriam, the very HER that the story tainted with the name of prostitute was, instead, the GREAT MOTHER.

The GREAT MOTHER that Yeshua loved deeply. He trusted her as much as he trusted himself. And in HER he recognized the Great Master that Myriam has always been since the ORIGIN of time.

He knew that after two thousand years it would be the feminine energy to welcome the masculine energy and that the two forces, in the name of the Rose, would finally UNITE, returning to the original pact of the Human Creation. He also knew that in the Divine-Human this Cosmic Marriage would never be outside oneself in a Couple but inside Oneself in its own CUP.

Those who follow themselves are not afraid of death or life. Those who follow their own feelings LIVE in Eternity!"

The *Circular Room* that hosts us and in which we continue to explore like a spiral begins to spin rapidly: old beliefs shatter in thousands of pieces, everything collapses and crumbles, an earthquake of emotions makes old knowledge rubble, while in the lukewarm water of the Mother's womb the ink of the old story melts. A deep unconditional love cradles us, a universal sound vibrates, changing the frequency of each of our cells. Intersecting helixes of strands of Gold awaken, as memories in Present Time unfold.

Mary, beautiful in her infinite Light, continues to speak to us about the Mother:

"Mother is not she who gave birth. Mother is she who gives birth to herself. She who gives birth is the mother of her children. The Mother is the one who gives birth to her own life.

The GREAT MOTHER is the one who gives birth to herself in every moment. The MOTHER is mother and father of herself and for this reason also a FATHER who within himself has found his GODDESS is a great MOTHER.

The Great Mother is the one who frees her own children by letting them go their own way, children who are not only those she gave birth to but also all the LOVED people.

Their journey is not Yours, and Your journey is not theirs.

No one can block the flow of a soul during its journey on Earth.

Your task as a Mother, for you who have given birth, is to be the BRIDGE between the earthly life and the Astral life. Loving, Growing, Nurturing when a child still does not recognize his needs, this is the joyful task of a Mother, but as soon as the uniqueness of his soul begins to remember, letting him go on his journey. This is true childbirth: letting him go on his soul's journey. This is the real GIFT.

This is one of the important messages I have come to give on Earth.

My beloved son experienced his journey, and many are the experiences he lived to recognize his Mastery. Traditional writings have never talked about his inner journey because this would have awakened the Consciousness of the Gods on Earth. They obscured the details to confuse the search for You.

Breathe, breathe soul companion, breathe . . . do not let anger trap you in the old. Breathe the New, the past is past, stay

in the present. The game of humanity served to assist humans to Ascend while remaining in the body.

Human evolution is like giving birth; it can sometimes be painful. But immediately after giving birth, when the creature smiles at the Great Mother, the pain is transformed in an instant, just as it happens to You today. The pain that you experienced in seeking the Divine, life after life, often brought you much suffering, but now looking into your eyes, seeing Your happy soul that smiles at you, in an instant everything is Transformed and the pain that preceded love surrenders.

In the detachment from our beloved Yeshua, both Myriam and I wept and suffered, but the pain was nothing in the face of the JOY and love that we felt in our hearts for having physically had him inside us. Me as a MOTHER, she as BRIDE. Women who love a man deeply both experience a deep symbiosis. The mother feels it when her child is in her womb; the beloved feels it when she unites with him physically. In healthy love both experience the orgasm, that in pure love becomes Cosmic.

Are you wondering when love is healthy?

When you love Yourself first.

When you love YOURSELF before Me.

When you love the other without loving yourself, you are not loving; you are looking for love.

Love is healthy when you LOVE the other without possessing.

The GODDESS unites not binds.

The Mother and the Bride are the bridge between the astral and the physical world: the first to bring the consciousness from the SPIRIT to MATER, to the MATTER, the other to bring man from the MATER, from the MATTER, to the SPIRIT. Through the Creative Energy, man reunites with God.

This is the Cosmic orgasm.

Love Yourself, and you will be able to LOVE.

Love Yourself, and beyond whether You are a Man or a Woman, you will be able to awaken Your being MOTHER.

I know that in the becoming of Timeless Time, like a refrain of out-of-tune music, the belief in the pain of the suffering Mother—the pain of death, sacrifice, drama, and the separation between the figure of Me and that of Myriam—created a dense web of conflicts trapping you in a ocean of fears.

The separation between Me and Magdalene altered the information of the VIRGIN, MOTHER, and of the PROSTITUTE WOMAN. It distracted and confused the human by separating him from his own soul. The human sought out that strong lack of self, and the man in the physical sense often sought both figures in two different women. Many men sought in the wife, the mother, and in the passionate lover, the woman Magdalene. A continuous search for the Void of love. A continuous struggle between the misunderstood dichotomy of the feminine and masculine energy. A spasmodic search for lost feminine energy.

Give it the name you want: Magdalene, Isis, Mother, Bride, Queen. The SOUL is always HER, the silent feminine energy that in very distant times surrendered to the masculine energy, separating from it. This separation dirtied the Sacredness of the Sexual Creative Energy, making vulgar what is Sacred and Sin what is Miracle.

The dormant human has forgotten his own ORIGIN from which he himself CREATES life.

MOTHER, You are the Miracle!

I invite you to Love Yourself.

How many times have you asked Me for the miracle, forgetting Yourself?

How many times have you sacrificed Yourself to look like me?

How many times have you silenced your pain?

MOTHER, LOVE YOURSELF!

A Mother cannot raise a child if she does not Love herself first. She cannot Understand a daughter if she does not Understand herself first. She cannot Welcome if she does not know how to Welcome herself. She cannot Respect if she does not know how to Respect herself.

She will transmit her infected fears from her own story.

Sacrifice, as you were taught, generates a sense of guilt, not Love.

Loving Oneself, giving birth to Oneself, this is to be a MOTHER!

The best gift you can give to a child is LOVING YOURSELF.

This is the eternal legacy.

Now, in the light of the New Awareness, do you understand that no MOTHER has faults?

The mother who did not give you love could not because she did not receive it. Nobody can give what he does not have. Nobody can take you where he has not gone.

Do you understand Now that everything was perfect?

Everything was an experience to get here, NOW, in the Time of Creation.

Mother, in my time on Earth, I let my son be born, I let my son live his earthly journey, I let my son reflect himself in his own light. Of this I have neither merits nor faults. This was his journey.

I left my MASTERY to me, the one that YOU recognize today in YOU!"

A talkative silence descends deep within us. Words seem to no longer make sense. Only the Silence of the heart speaks and transforms our frequency, while the New Awareness gradually becomes a beacon in the center of our eyes.

The strength and the Mastery of Mary amaze us, enrapture us, silence us.

She who in the collective imagination has been imbued with drama and suffering, smilingly concludes:

"*Being reborn in You, remaining in the same body, this is the Mastery of the New Time. Being aware that You are the miracle, this is the Mastery of the New Time. Recognizing that You are God-Goddess who Creates, this is the Mastery of the New Time.*"

In the name of the Rose, so it is.

Mother

Anima

Radiant

Infinitely

Adores

7

The Water

With Gentle Grace I address you, and with the *sound* of water I introduce myself to You. Water Woman. Water Mother. Water Life. The water contained in Your every cell. The Source water.

Inexhaustible Divine Source in which you lived in the Sacred bridge. Inexhaustible Divine Source in which you lived even before being a Divine-Human. Your every cell overflows with water, and in this moment of great change on the planet, the sound of your water transmutes your existence. The water of Your cells is infused with new information, and this, imbued with your new sound, transmutes the events of your life.

Pay attention to the transparency of the water in your cells.

Your water receives from You. Give it Love, Yours.

Let it flow, Master . . .

Learn to feel the vibration of Your water and,

with love for you, become the informer it dips into.

With love learn to observe Your thoughts. Listen to the *sound* of Your emotions. These are the ones that brighten or pollute Your water. Anger, fear, guilt, pollute the water of Your cells. I am not telling you not to feel these emotions. I remind you to welcome them in your Grail, and in the Sacred Cup, I urge you to observe them. Observing does not mean judging them.

Observe, listen, allow yourself to feel how you feel in your belly. I urge you to Listen to yourself in the depths of Your water. This is what creates your life. Thanks to the information from water, You remember who you Are.

Soul companion . . .

Why would you have chosen water to live in Your mother's womb?

Why would you have chosen to live in a matter made almost entirely of water?

Why would you have chosen to live on a planet almost entirely covered with water?

How do you think Energy circulates in Your body if not through water?

Your heart, the engine of your human experience, carries your water to every part of you. When I speak of the heart I am not speaking of the cardiac organ; I am speaking of the metaphysical heart. This is where the Sacredness of Your water is kept. When Your inner water is polluted, every part of You is polluted. When Your water is transparent, every part of You is transparent. The quality of the water that is in You is the vibration that You emanate. It is Your *sound*. It is what You Are.

Let it flow . . . let it happen.

As Above, so Below, water is PRESENCE.

They made you believe you were born with SIN, and to become INNOCENT they baptized you with water, cleaning you from a GUILT that you never earned.

Soul companion . . . You are INNOCENT! You are INNOCENT!

Your body, Your spirit is INNOCENT, and the only water you can immerse yourself in to get Baptized is the love that flows in Your heart. In the coming times there will still be many discoveries of water in the womb of the Great Mother, many of these will help you to remember. The water CODES will be revealed, and many of them will awaken what has always been kept in Your DNA. In the coming times water in all forms will take away a lot of waste from the planet, and water, in the micro and macro, will be increasingly transparent. Surrender to the purity of Your Spirit. Quench Your body and let every sip of water be a prayer. The PRAYER that comes from the awareness of who you are, not from the dogma you have been taught, in that there is Power not LOVE.

Breathe . . . Breathe . . . Breathe . . . Let it happen . . .

Breathe and remember . . .

Water is by its nature infinite and comes to You to

remind you of Your infinite being in the Earth of the Kristic Sun. When I speak of the Kristic Sun, I am not speaking of a Kristic figure, I am speaking of a frequency. The same frequency that the water of a CRYSTAL has when it is pure. Pure means without information from the past. Pure means ORIGIN. Num Posa Pedre, Lam Siri Om.

IN THE AKASHIC ROOMS

Bathed in the essence of her love, Myriam invites us to immerse ourselves in the Sacred Waters.

"In this akashic space it will be the water of your own soul that will Baptize you," she tells us, while infinite drops of crystalline water bathe her face, making it even fresher and more graceful. Everything flows, waterfalls, streams, jets of transparent water streaked with delicate brushstrokes of blue. A sight never seen before. With refined sweetness she asks us if we are ready to let ourselves go to the frequency of what has no form.

"Water is sound," she adds.

"Water is sound."

With closed eyes our inner vision is amplified, our pineal gland is freed, and in the lukewarm crystalline water of the frequency that we emanate, our Consciousness stops.

"Where are we?" Joy asks.

From the Crystal companion of our journey, the echo of an answer.

"*You are in your Body, you are in your Blood, you are in your Temple.*"

With the joyful heart of a child exploring life, the experience takes shape.

"It is wonderful to be inside and outside at the same time. This is magic!"

"*No,*" Myriam replies.

"*This is not magic. This is the Consciousness of the New Energy that You have Created.*"

Like a beacon in the night, Myriam's frequency guides us, hand in hand, to the source of our water. Similar to a courtship of love, our relationship with every part of our body begins to form. The Temple of the soul feels welcomed in its sovereignty. Every organ has its own music; every cell has its history. Water is the Divine Presence, is the information, the action that takes shape inside You.

Action comes from a Thought.

Thought comes from a Belief.

Belief comes from a Loan.

"A loan?" Joy asks, amazed.

"*Yes, a loan. A loan from someone who informed You through his belief, gave You the form of his thought, You believed it was Yours, and with it you gave shape to Your experiences. The water of Your every cell is imbued with information you believed to be Yours. Every organ has obeyed, at times it has even suffered.*"

Breathe, breathe deeply, breathe there, in the depths of

Your belly, let the warmth of your breath bring you back to the essence. Breathe without doing. Just be Breath. Allow yourself to breathe in the water of Your cells, observe that water, and in the talkative silence of your heart listen to the voice of your conscience that speaks to You . . .

"*How did you learn to love in life?*"

Respond quickly, do not allow thoughts to obscure the vision of Your water. Whatever is the answer, it is okay. Do not judge anything, just be aware of the information imbued in the water of Your Cells. Like water let this question flow through You . . .

"*How did you learn to love in life?*"

Breathe . . . take your time.

Breathe, breathe and listen . . .

In the New Akashic Rooms Your water flows. It is transparent. There is no echo of old perceptions, where existence after existence you had to keep the old *imprinting*. Now everything is New; Now it is You who can choose to inform the water of Your cells of new frequencies. You no longer need Loans. You can use Your abundance and be the orchestra conductor of the music of Your thoughts. Every organ of Your body, with the information that You choose to give to Your water, will play another music, and by changing the score it will accord with the Sound of Origin.

"*How did you learn to love in life?*"

Answer from your belly. Answer with Your voice . . .

Whatever the answer, know that it is perfect. It is perfect

because it is yours. And no one, except yourself, can judge it.

Soul companion . . .

You were just *dormant,* not wrong. You were just *unaware,* not guilty.

In the first years of Your life, you learned to love through the filters they transmitted to you, information borrowed from someone who in turn borrowed it from someone else. This information lacked the frequency of love for You. Now in the New Time, You know that someone had no faults. He simply did not know because he himself was a program tampered with by the occult power.

Breathe . . . breathe . . . breathe . . . soul companion . . .

Breathe in the presence of You. Ask your consciousness: "How did I learn to love in life?"

By satisfying the needs of the other?

By submitting myself?

Through victimhood?

By worrying about others?

By attracting attention?

By believing I was wrong?

By obeying religious dogmas?

By delegating to the other?

"How did I learn to love? How did I learn to love myself? And what did I learn about love?"

Answer from the belly. Answer with your voice.

Whatever the answer, know that it is perfect.

The awareness comes from love not from judgment.

The information that in the first place polluted the purity of the water of the Divine-Human cells is that of having believed to be wrong, that of having believed to be a SINNER. Another polluting message is that the devil is the antithesis of the Divine and has, through the frequency of separation, dirtied the water with the seed of FEAR, thus giving rise to an invasive and festering belief:

"I AM NOT WORTHY."

This belief is the source of guilt, which in every form manifests itself with drama and has deprived you of your ENJOYMENT of life.

When I speak of Enjoyment, I speak of the awareness of being Divine as well as Human, both without ANY separation.

"My fault, my fault, my very great fault." Here is the matrix of separation.

Beating your chest with this accusation has done nothing but alter the rhythm of your heart, informing the water in your cells of a SIN that you have never committed.

It's not your FAULT that Yeshua died!

Water, informed of false beliefs, being the conductor of physical matter, continued to transmit information to every cell, to every organ, and, therefore, to every experience. Here, the sound of Origin remained buried in the pineal tabernacle and waited. A waiting that lasted more than two thousand years. A waiting reinforced by ambivalent information, which baptized with the water of the occult belief further sealed the illusion of the dormant.

The ritual of Baptism, lived with awareness and presence, is one of the most beautiful experiences that can be given to a newborn baby, but there is no SIN he needs to clean himself of. It is a ceremony that welcomes the unborn child into the living water of information that will shape his future of love for life not of drama and much less of lies by the occult power.

The Sacred Water in the Baptism of the New Time takes away the past and with it all the beliefs and information that have distanced the human from his own soul. It is the mirror in which the soul recognizes her purity. She cleans the water of every cell, a purge that rids this infestation of beliefs. She flows like a river taking away every ancient karma, every ancient perception of past lives, and every lie on the part of the occult.

Water is that which has no form, just like the soul before entering her vessel.

It is in the Water that the human remembers the sound of ORIGIN.

It is in the Water that the Divine-Human immerses himself and feels himself to Be WATER.

It is in the Water informed of the frequency of INNOCENCE that Myriam invites to immerse ourselves in the womb of the Great Mother:

In the Presence and with the Power of my soul.
Aware of being pure Consciousness.

I immerse myself in the womb of the GREAT MOTHER.

I immerse myself in the Sacred Water of the ancient Wisdom of Isis.

I bless the journey of my existence and with water Informed of the frequency of Innocence I choose to open the SEAL that was closed to me by the occult power so as not to REMEMBER who I was. With the water of the GREAT MOTHER, I free my mind from all the thoughts I have borrowed that have made me believe I Am Guilty.

I free myself from the belief in SIN, and with all the love I feel for myself, I bless the path of my existence on the planet of water.

Num Posa Pedre, Lam Siri Om.

In the Name of the Rose, so it is.

8
The Truth
Always Comes Out

The truth always comes out.

Do not hide it. Do not deny it. Do not disguise it.

They did so with me. This has caused the Divine-Human lack, suffering, and separation. Now Everything is done. I breathe in Your breath. I love in Your heart. I live through Your Experiences, and You live to become aware of who you are. The truth is the human in the womb of the Goddess; after his cycle it is natural that he comes to Light. Like a butterfly that emerges, after maturing in a chrysalis, the truth breaks the veil to be FREE. Yes, free from what still separates You from Your soul.

The truth is the Freedom of Your soul.

Do not feel guilty. You don't need it.

Do not judge yourself. You don't need it.

Do not think you are not worthy. You don't need it.

Instead, listen to Your soul fully and welcome the fear that still makes you lie. Embrace the fear that still does not make you completely Yourself.

Surrender to Your Soul.

Let your weary "I" surrender to its death. In this way you will not need a physical death, but what you no longer need and that still separates you from Your Divinity will die in You.

If Yourself is tired, let it free.

Free it from the control. Free it from manipulation. Free it from what is not Yours. Free it from your needs, from anger. Free it from guilt, from judgment. Free it of its fragility.

Do not beautify your prison by believing yourself free.

Get out of your prison and fly FREE.

Resign yourself. FREEDOM is Your DESTINY, and You are destined for PURE LOVE.

IN THE AKASHIC ROOMS

A fresh and clean scent attracts our senses; the feeling of being back home pervades us in every cell. Welcomed by the thousand arms of the Goddess of Compassion, we feel very at ease in the New Akashic Room. An infinite light accompanied by a deep breath opens the curtain to the one who in every moment reminds us of the breath of the Vital Circle.

Sitting next to Myriam, Kuan Yin appears in her beauty. In their eyes signs of eternal complicity mark the Timeless

Time. Almond petals create soft rugs on which mirrors of light reflect the symbol of infinity. Similar to a hologram, its phosphorescent colors and myriad shapes enchant us.

In this *Circular Room* the Light is truly dazzling.

Quietly, without anyone noticing it, a limiting thought demands attention, distracting us from our CENTER.

"But won't all this Light be too much?" Joy asks.

Suddenly, a loud roar, the golden dust that characterizes the *Circular Room* seems to become sand in the desert on a windy night. Ancient voices speak strange indecipherable languages. A strong vortex seems to suck us in. Colors darken. The smells stink of old. For a few breaths, the scenery before our eyes seems to have changed.

Fear stops the Light.

"What is happening?" Joy screams in fright.

Myriam smiles and observes.

Her bright face is caressed by her auburn hair. Nothing disrupts her. Her strength and her Mastery remain firm in the Center of her chest.

"What is happening? I am scared! I am scared!" Joy, sweating with tears, continues to scream.

"Here it is . . . This is the face of love when it forgets itself and disguises itself as FEAR," Myriam replies.

"How? Does Love disguise itself as fear? It is not possible, love cannot disguise itself. And why should it do that?"

"AND YOU who ARE LOVE, why do you continue to disguise yourself with what you are not?

*The truth always comes out and WHAT YOU ARE can
no longer be hidden.*

Love is YOU, naked of Your old memories."

A heartfelt silence expands, and the desire to know the
new is affirmed.

Myriam and Kuan Yin, looking into each other's eyes,
caress each other in the thin veils of the soul. The Goddess
of Compassion invites us to take our breath into the depths
of the belly.

*"The center of your body is a point that remembers, thinks,
and acts autonomously. The human believes that everything
dwells in the cells of his brain and often forgets to let the breath
flow into the brain of his belly: this is where fear hides. In the
mystical amygdala, however, there are traces of ancient memories, very often of previous lives."*

"Previous lives? Kuan Yin, explain yourself better," Joy
asks, his eyes wide with amazement.

*"The amygdala is closely linked to the sixth energetic
body. Thanks to this link the old Akasha archived memories
in the universal library. There is now no PAST-based information in the Circular Rooms of Creation. There is no more
information based on FEAR. Instead, there are ENERGIES
that are gradually taking shape in ways that, for now, are
still UNIMAGINABLE for you. This is because these are
ENERGIES that go BEYOND the linear mind. These go
BEYOND the old belief systems that until now you have
known and that life after life you have kept as your perception*

of the world. These, on an unconscious level, have been the cause of the lack of Divine realization on Earth. In the New Time, Spirituality is concrete not abstract. Spirituality must be applied not theorized. Spirituality has nothing to do with religion.

The fear of ascending on Earth and discovering that you are CREATORS is the greatest test for humans to overcome.

Now, everything is happening thanks to the return of the Feminine strength. The Mater's Creative Power returns the Grail of his Eternal Divinity to the human."

Kuan Yin smiles and crosses the light of Myriam's deep eyes, who, nodding, hints at an accomplice smile. Silence, amazement, and New Awareness blossoms. The new Earth is fertile, and everything seems to grow very fast.

"Before arriving at the Time of Creation you lived many experiences as dormants: everything was perfect, none of them were wrong. These were the various stops that on the day of the initial promise you agreed to make, knowing that you would arrive at the ascension on Earth. Now in the New Time, in the Time of Awakening, the New Circular Rooms have changed, in them there is neutral ENERGY, not ancient memory. There is fresh energy, not past memories.

The only FEAR that can block the human for a little while is surrendering to the UNIMAGINABLE.

THE UNIMAGINABLE.

Breathe, breathe soul companion . . .

Breathe and know that things will happen in a simple and

new way, in a way that humans do not yet know because it is information that comes from the infinite worlds, not from memories. The new Akashic pages are written by the New Energy; they are written in the DNA of the Divine-Human who has awakened, aware of being the Creator of his own life. He lives it without suffering it anymore through the power of fear.

FEAR is the SOURCE of all discomforts.

The soul is not afraid, the soul does not fear, does not judge, does not control. The soul is compassionate. The truth of the soul always comes out."

"Myriam, what is the truth?" Joy asks excitedly.

"The truth is not only the falsehood, the lie, and everything that has been occulted for centuries. The truth is also the courage to be sincere with Yourself. It is not the lie you tell the other; it is the lie you tell Yourself.

The truth is to surrender yourself to being completely What You Are. It is remembering the PROMISE made to Your soul. With Her, you can procrastinate as much as you want, but in the end, for that ancient pact, you will have to give yourself to HER."

Wrapped in the softness of a white dress, Myriam catches our bewildered, even amazed look. Wonder accompanies us, and the Master breath supports our natural Transformation.

"The truth is to surrender to your Divine nature. It is surrendering yourself to the I Am, not to the infinite lives you have lived previously. Those are the experiences of your infinite ASPECTS. Now in the New Time of Awakening, you unite piece by piece, bringing your consciousness back to its unified

origin. Those experiences are the acts of a long theatrical comedy, thanks to which you have been able to interpret the various characters to really discover who you Are. They have helped you to arrive in the New Time and gain the New Awareness of what Your purpose as a Divine-Human really is. You do not have to save anyone: this is not your task, nor your mission. Your purpose is to UNIFY your consciousness as it was in the ORIGIN. In the Eternal Consciousness Your task is to Love and Enjoy the beauty of Your Divine being in the MATTER.

Yes, the MATTER.

When You are love without speaking of love anymore, the other will remember who HE IS. When You do what you do for JOY and not for mission, the other will awaken his JOY of living. You do not need to protect yourself from anything. The Frequency that a Master emanates annihilates any past with his own PRESENCE, not through what he says but through his Present Being. Let yourself be guided by the Masters who Are what they say, not by those who tell you how to be. Let yourself be guided by the Masters who look at you in the eyes, reminding you Who You Are. The incarnated Master does not tell you what to do; he is what he says. He feeds on himself, and he will help You feed on Yourself.

A beacon sheds light as a beacon not because somebody chooses to follow it.

You who are listening at this moment are an ancient soul. You have already experienced everything you needed to live to get here.

At the origin of Your journey on Earth, you made Your promise, and with love in Your every existence, you left your vessel, but you have always carried HER with You—the promise of arriving at the Time of Awakening.

Now you are here! You have reached that point: surrender to the UNIMAGINABLE.

Trust and acknowledge to Yourself that you were fundamental for this epochal change. Yes, You who accused yourself, criticized yourself many times, believing yourself unworthy and believing you were wrong. You did not do anything wrong; you just did not know.

Not knowing you remained in the prison of FEAR, and this is the mother of the emotions of Your belly.

Where there is anger there is FEAR.

Where there is a sense of guilt there is FEAR.

Where there is judgment there is FEAR.

Where there is jealousy there is FEAR.

Where there is envy there is FEAR.

Where there is FEAR there is no LOVE.

In the past you have chosen to hold these emotions close to You by holding them in your hands like glass fragments. You cut yourself with the pain of the past, staining the whiteness of Your conscience. Because of this memory, you were forced to return each time with new vessels. NOW is no longer time. Now you die to be reborn in your own body, with Your soul finally breathing within You, letting the Spirit free to live with no more past.

Love is what You Are; fear is what others have taught you.

Fear makes you keep things the way they have always been; love makes you see things as they can be.

Surrender, give yourself to Your soul. The truth always comes out. FREEDOM is Your Eternal Consciousness. LOVE is Your Destiny.

Breathe . . . breathe . . .

Breath is Presence.

Breath is Now.

Breath is Simple."

A new sensation accompanies us in the silence of the VOID. The friendly crystal reveals new secrets to us, and our ability to CREATE begins to intrigue us. Our breathing has changed.

The Goddess of Compassion, before greeting us, invites us to have compassion toward ourselves, smiles, and silently disappears, leaving the trail of her maternal perfume. Myriam *blows* in our heart, and the talkative silence travels together with our Consciousness, which, similar to a spiral, continues to Expand . . .

Everything is New.

ALL IS! REALLY AMAZING!

In the name of the Rose, so it is.

9

You Are What You Are

With Gentle Grace to You I come, and with Sweet Firmness I speak to You.

From then to NOW I Return. From then to NOW I Remain.

The occult no longer has Power. My Presence is Everywhere. It is Tangible. It is Present. The Eternal Consciousness of Me expands, and the human, in the becoming of his awakening, gradually remembers.

Have you ever wondered why you always had a deep love for me?

Have you ever wondered why you have always looked for me over the centuries?

Breathe, breathe soul companion . . . breathe and listen.

Through the search for me You were looking for YOURSELF.

Many of you who are now listening to these words have recognized my frequency because you too were there with me in those Places and Times. Many of you have accompanied me, many have betrayed me, many have abandoned me. But many more, you have Loved me deeply.

Many of you, Cathars, Templars, in the becoming of the centuries, life after life, you have returned. . . . The pure in heart have always Loved and Venerated me like the Male Kristic Seed. The occult power feared this, and the hooded ones buried the bodies under the Earth. That Living Earth that today *speaks*. That Sacred Earth that today *remembers*.

Nothing can Be buried when it is true.

My Kristic Presence now Returns and radiates the minds of those who, *in the name of the Rose,* RE-awaken.

My Kristic Presence now Returns and radiates hearts that cry tears of Joy for having waited and believed in my Return.

My LOVE is Passion; it is a River in Flood. They will be overwhelmed by it, those who, through the golden flame of their hearts, choose to Transform the old, and with the water that comes in all forms in these times, they will baptize the NEW.

With Gentle Grace and Sweet Firmness I breathe to You . . .

Open Your heart wide, renew your thoughts.

Your heart is Yours; your thoughts are not.

Your heart is the place where Your soul dwells.

You Are What You Are.

Now I ask you: In the New Time what does it mean to you to Find me again?

Divine soul I do not come to You to be VENERATED in prayer with hands joined. I Am Frequency and I am in You every time You Unite with Yourself. Every time you become aware of who you are. Your strength, Your dignity, Your sweetness, Your innate ability to recognize Your archaic Mastery, Your Passion, the Joy of living, all this was already Yours before my coming on Earth, but the occult, sealing Your Secret Eye, like a magic potion, stunned your mind and confused your heart, making you believe in Suffering, in Sacrifice, in the Drama of the heavy Cross.

Tender companion, New Masculine awakening, I Return in You and in the Sweetness of Your Feminine Strength I Breathe. Welcome me. Make room and allow yourself to breathe in Your new gaze that dawn after dawn clears up from the fear of love.

YOU ARE WHAT YOU ARE.

Identification, this is what I now want to talk to you about.

Yes. It is the identification that separated you from Yourself.

Every time you add more next to the I AM, you are separating yourself.

Every time you add a title next to the I AM, you are separating yourself.

I Am a vegetarian; I Am a Buddhist; I Am a naturalist; I

Am angry; I Am incapable and infinitely many. I AM.

You feel anger: you are not angry. It is different. Whenever you say I AM ANGRY, you are identifying with the emotion of anger and making it yours through the memory of the Body.

Try to experience it now.

Say I AM ANGRY.

Observe and listen to your body.

Now say IN THIS MOMENT I FEEL ANGER.

You will see that the experience will be completely different. In this way the emotion will remain conscious and will not become embedded in the memory of your body.

This is the same every time you say I AM VEGETARIAN. You made the choice to eat LIVE food. It is different. To affirm I AM VEGETARIAN is to identify yourself in a group, and you are not a group. You ARE YOU! Identification is a cage, the I am, while I live this or that experience is freedom.

The truth is me who lives the Human Experience.

I AM!

The soul has no labels, no signs stuck on the forehead with the mark of the occult. Every time you add something else to the I Am, it becomes polluted with what you Are not.

The Spirit IS.

The Soul IS.

The Heart IS.

The I AM must be lived, not intellectualized.

In the I AM that awakens, the Master who Ascends on Earth takes Shape.

Pay attention to the sound you use to divulge who you Are.

What is the sound? That is the word. And the word is a sound.

The sound is frequency. YOURS.

Try to change the sound, and Your melody will change Your Reality. Every time you affirm I Am and add more, you are separating yourself. There is a judgment, which, as in the religions, makes use of absolute truth.

If your profession is to be a doctor and you feel strong in asserting "I am a doctor," ask yourself, "Who Am I without a white coat?" If your profession is to be a teacher and you feel strong in asserting "I am a teacher," ask yourself, "Who Am I without a desk?"

We could go on indefinitely. You live that experience; you are not that experience. You Are pure Consciousness. Period.

You Are What You Are. Everything else is the soul playing in life. Let her play. Let the Passion expand. Let the Passion, as the one that existed between me and Yeshua, take Shape in the Purity of love.

I and Yeshua are the frequency of the UNION, and in the Eternal Present it is through this that we live in You.

Now and Forever. Always and Forever in the Grail, I welcome you, and raising it to your Mastery I Support your ascension on Earth.

IN THE AKASHIC ROOMS

The smell of fire intrigues our sense of smell. In the crackle of the flames, centuries of mystery burn infinite bodies. In the New Akashic Rooms there is no smell of burnt skin but only visions of golden ash. The smell of fire is no longer that of burning meat but of the I Am that asserts itself. The heat warms our hands; in them archaic symbols are revealed in their frequency alternating respectfully, first one, then the other. We are amazed by the color of the fire: it is a deep purple. Without any resistance, we choose to let ourselves be Transformed.

Everything is clear. In the experience that we are going to have, something very strong awaits us. Not just something, maybe even someone. Who?

The new akashic space is ablaze with ancestral truths. The fire burns with intense passion. The air smells of lilies, and the sensation we experience is the same as when expecting an important guest.

The echo of a melody attracts our attention:

"In the New Energy there is no past that holds back. There is a PRESENT that welcomes."

With pleasure we remember that this is what we were told before entering the New Akashic Rooms. The authentic desire to open up to the New is amplified, even if a slight fear seems to be willing to stay a little longer in our company.

Fear.

Fear of what?

Fear of the new?

Fear of the unknown?

Afraid of knowing who is the guest of this new SPACE?

We neither know nor try to understand. Without judging we welcome in our hearts that part of us that vacillates in fear, and by feeding it with our love it reassures itself.

We let ourselves go in a deep breath . . .

The Crystal companion of our journey, through its Kristic radiance reminds us of ours.

Yet another deep BREATH, and the desire to expand into the new brings us back to the CENTER.

Myriam welcomes us with her penetrating gaze, allowing us to look into the antiquity of her deep eyes, revealing symbols of ancient lives.

Her voice is a sound . . .

"'Many lives and many tasks await you' my beloved told me that day when my eyes met his gaze. I suffered a lot for him and for what had happened, but he too suffered for me because he already knew what would have happened next.

We both had OUR JOURNEY and the PROMISE made to our soul with whom we had agreed to experience the becoming of our existence on Earth.

God, how I suffered when I could no longer touch or caress him, when my mouth stopped kissing his lips. How hard it was for me to surrender to the detachment from his physical body. I missed the smell of his body terribly, but his constant and silent presence very soon silenced in me the human part. He

knew that the thorns embedded in his head would be the thorns of the white roses that every woman, through her own blood, would have to recognize before awakening to her own Creative Power."

"Myriam, what do you mean? What thorns are you talking about?" asks Joy.

Myriam remains silent; for the first time her eyes fill with tears. In that moment we realize how much her shining eyes make her even more beautiful. Silence. Only a respectful silence. This is what we are able to give her.

Like a free horse by the sea, our heart begins to gallop. Compassion toward a Woman who for the first time we saw as frail in her Human garment is the New Experience we are having.

Her tears begin to flow down the cheeks of her clear face. Beautiful. Beautiful of infinite beauty, her crimson dress that day is moistened with the innocent water of her tears. The wet fabric shows her soft breasts, while the delicacy of her skin and the frequency of her love inebriates our senses without the need to add any words.

Respectfully we remain silent. A talkative silence, a silence that lets only the heart speak in the beating of its breath. The movement of the belly sways in and out of us. The crunch of the exuberant fire plays its melody.

Fear? Amazement? Loss?

We cannot immediately understand what it is, but suddenly Myriam's body seems to double; sharp and clear figures appear before our eyes. Now there are two Women.

Joan with her sweet pride is there.

"Joan? But . . . but . . . are you?"

Myriam, with the complicity of someone who knows, smiles at Joan, revealing a deep emotion. With the eyes of love, the two women continue to admire each other for a long time. Joan lets herself go in a deep maternal embrace, finally allowing herself to express her feminine strength without masking herself in a hard armor.

An indescribable emotion, difficult to shape through words.

The fire of the flame meanwhile continues to burn.

In the beauty of her young age, the maid is before our eyes. Myriam, letting her scarf embrace her, delicately moves away as if to emphasize the woman who, as natural as a flower, is ready to let her truth blossom.

Joan begins to take off her masculine clothes. Inside the hard armor a soft woman's body begins to take shape. Her small and delicate breasts seem to want to be given permission to relax without the fear of being crushed and hidden. Her belly allows itself to breathe its venerable roundness. With a liberating and elegant gesture, she pulls the hat of her shaggy short hair from her head, and auburn strands fall softly down her sensual back, which appears more and more feminine.

She takes off every garment down to the last, leaving her body completely naked. Joan, turning to the left, directs her gaze toward the crackle of the FIRE, which continues to burn. She stares at that fire for a long time, her eyes filled with tears, first wetting her face and then her body, until they reach those flames that, thanks to the water of her own tears, begin to go out. A smell of wet earth awakens our sense of smell, while Myriam with a pure white sheet comes to meet Joan, wrapping her delicate body in a warm embrace.

She gently strokes her face and says:

"I know who you are, Joan. You Are an aspect of me, You are me . . . LET YOURSELF go . . . It is no longer time to fight. It is no longer time to struggle . . . Let yourself go."

Like children expecting to be enchanted by a fairy tale, we huddle around her to listen. We thought to hear a story with dates and places, kings and horses. We are soon amazed when Joan starts talking to us about something that takes us far *beyond* what we knew about her.

Myriam goes away for the second time, and with a deep respect for Joan, she remains silent. Joan with infinite Grace continues to enrapture us with her presence:

"When I was in Myriam's vessel, Yeshua told me that there would be many lives that awaited me, but I did not understand at the time. Many will be the bodies of women who will be burned by the flames of fear; for many years the creative force heralding the truth will be stained with blood. Many will be the women who, life after life, will sacrifice their bodies, but NO fire will ever be able to burn their soul.

This will be the journey thanks to which humanity will surrender to its Creative Power, and in the feminine strength, inherent in the human, it will recognize itself."

"But why? Why?" Joy asks, strangled by emotion.

"It is no longer time to ask why. It is no longer time to know the truth about the King that I helped in that experience. It is no longer time to understand why my struggle was against the English people. Of course, I loved France deeply: above all I wanted to thank her. I felt grateful to her for the infinite love received. That land had really loved me so much."

In that moment Joan turns her complicit gaze toward Myriam who, albeit in the distance, was there always PRESENT.

"But why, why dress up as a soldier? Why deny your being feminine?"

"Because this was what the feminine strength needed to experience before reaching the Time of Awakening. Humanity, confused in its masculine and feminine forces, in its light and shadow aspects, above and below, good and bad, has created war as a mirror of its own duality. But it is thanks to the creation of duality that it was able to recognize itself.

What I experienced then is what many humans have done by denying their Creative Power. There are many women who throughout history have believed in the power of masculine strength and have fought with it, unaware of just how much this was a false strength that separated them from their soul.

One is not a woman by imitating a man. One is a WOMAN, remaining a WOMAN.

In that experience I was conflicted, caught in a fight between what I felt and what I did. The Divine voice that spoke to me sometimes made me believe I was insane. This also happened to the many who started to awaken, began to 'hear' the voice of their own consciousness, and who often believed it was just a fragile insanity. I wore the male armor as a mask that enabled me to fight; I did not know that only by listening to my soul could I really win. I was apparently fighting against a people and for a male, a king, who later betrayed me in the visible real world, embodying the story of the one who betrayed me.

It is never the other who betrays; the other is just a mirror. The rational masculine actually wanted to reveal to the apparently betrayed human that the masculine is little compared to the wisdom of the human's creative soul and that it would be his rational masculine that would betray him in his evolution.

Apparently, I was fighting against the English, but in reality I was fighting my fear of fully listening to the Divine inner voice that spoke to me. I fought with my body, which reminded me that I was a woman and that it suffered a lot every time I imprisoned it in the hard shell of my mind. I fought with my will and desire to save my country at all costs, taking charge of everyone, forgetting that everyone has his own journey and that everyone has in himself the power to save himself.

Archetypally, who were the people I was fighting against? Who was I really fighting with?

They were the ASPECTS, the ASPECTS of myself through which I could experience.

The human has always believed he could fight with or against someone or something, but in reality through the other he has always fought against himself. Every human is born to have an inner experience, and this is not about history or data: it is about awareness.

When everything started at the Origin, there was the One, the Origin, Home. The Unified Consciousness.

From there consciousness separated into experience. The first separation was that of duality. The minute facts I experienced through Joan do not help the awakening of humanity. Studying dates, places, personal details stupefies the nonlinear mind, which the Divine-Human is discovering about himself.

The human already knows the experience of the I Am. Through duality he has forgotten it. In the Time of Awakening, he remembers who he is, and that is why in the New Akashic Rooms, it is no longer time to know the minute details of history but to go BEYOND history. It is not necessary to understand the history of humanity, but rather to know the history of Consciousness. In the Time of Creation this is what is needed.

The experience that my soul had through Joan was that of recognizing myself for what I was. I had to experience TRUST.

This was why in that prison, which was nothing but my mind, I doubted the voice of my Spirit speaking to me. The prison of my mind made me believe in defeat first and then madness. Later however, surrendering to the voice of my soul, I recognized within Me the clear experience of Trust.

It was there that I remembered the PROMISE.

Many women believed that by imitating men their power would prevail, but it did not. I in the guise of a man did not win a people, for many I was defeated, but in reality that was my VICTORY.

Allowing yourself to live your experience without judging yourself—this is victory.

In the Time of Awakening, it is no longer time for stakes, it is no longer time for fires, it is no longer time for thorns. What burns and transforms thanks to the fire of the Gold flame is the old duality turning into Mastery.

Now it is no longer the Time to feel anger at what has been; it is Time to love yourself for WHAT YOU ARE!

There are no more sins to atone for. You deserve love because this is You, because this is the choice you made by detaching yourself from the Origin. The fire that burned the bodies on those horrible stakes, turning them to ashes, left behind a message of fear in the old chronicle of the Akasha, and this fear sowed doubts, suppressing the connection with the soul. False perceptions were perpetuated, and the fear of being connected with the Divine became a habit of a select few. FEAR gave way to the armor of a rational masculine

who controls and supervises, thus putting the Creative Power to sleep.

The connection with one's Consciousness is the true secret of ascension. This is inherent in the human who upon awakening remembers the smell of Home. By remembering, he will no longer need to leave his body to ascend. He will remember his promise, and he will begin to grow warm with the heat of his own fire, no longer afraid of being burned.

The BATTLE between light and darkness is over. The shadow and the light are now integrated. The human no longer needs this experience. Whoever still believes in this will leave his body, and for him it will start over. For those, however, who are aware, this will accelerate the Enjoyment of their Mastery on Earth.

The human is ready to connect to the Center of Energy where there is no longer duality. It will not be like this for everyone. It will take a long time for all humans to have this full awareness.

Rejoice. The war is over! Beyond what they want him to believe, the human lives his best Times. The awakened human is no longer a dream: it is a reality. The human is allowing himself to truly love himself, recognizing his Creative Power of God-Goddess within himself.

Soul companion . . . Relax, relax.

Hang the armor on a nail and choose to truly be what You Are."

In the *Circular Rooms* the Breath becomes PRAYER.

Myriam and Joan enveloped in the flame of Kristic gold, UNITED, disappear . . . Magic becomes Mastery.

Consciousness is enriched with the nectar of experience.

In the Here and Now Everything is perfect.

Yes, Everything is really Perfect . . .

In the name of the Rose, so it is.

10

The Three D

With Gentle Grace to you I address, to You Divine power I introduce myself.

Here we are! The Time is NOW. The Time of the Three D has come to You!

Soul companion . . . I do not come to tell you: live your Divinity.

With Gentle Grace to YOU I come to tell you: You ARE your DIVINITY.

You have no more escape. You can no longer dress in tight clothes.

You can no longer remain ATTACHED to what YOU ARE not. You can no longer remain ATTACHED to the roles, identifications, emotions you feel, labels, thoughts of the collective consciousness of your family, your region, your nation. You can no longer remain ATTACHED to excuses from your past lives. You can no longer remain ATTACHED to the mass consciousness from which, when, unaware of who you Are, you let yourself be swallowed up.

NOW in the Time of the Three D, everything is ready.

The Time of the Three D contains the DETACHMENT.

The DETACHMENT?

From what? Detachment from whom?

The DETACHMENT from Yourself, Master.

NOW I know that Your linear mind is asking you: but what does it mean to detach myself from myself?

Breathe, Breathe, Master. Allow yourself the experience of feeling, stay listening and feel what DETACHMENT from Yourself is for you.

Breathe, Breathe and listen . . .

All of the work you have done as a Divine-Human since you walked through the wall of fire has been Magnificent. That work, which first generated a centrifugal movement and then centripetal, brought you to YOURSELF.

You have learned to Love yourself.

You have learned to Recognize yourself.

You have learned to Listen to yourself.

You have learned to stay in the Silence of Your Heart.

You have fought. You have faced demons and rivals. You have sweated, and with the shadow that often seemed dark to you, you have LIGHTENED the veil of your eyes gradually remembering who YOU ARE.

Now you KNOW. Now YOU ARE.

Now DETACH YOURSELF from YOURSELF!

You cannot EXPAND if you remain in the belief

that you are just What You Are only in this Existence.

You Are BEYOND. You Are OTHER. You are the WHOLE.

Your MULTIDIMENSIONAL JOURNEY has begun.

Your EXPANSION is in progress.

LIVE IT then! What are you waiting for?

SURRENDER!

RESIGN YOURSELF!

ENOUGH with the crumbs of awareness!

Enough BEGGING. Enough BEGGING for LOVE. Enough seeking Advice and Approval. Enough getting lost within the walls of the EGO.

If you have hung up JUDGMENT, GUILT, FEAR. Why do you turn back to look at them. What good is it?

ENOUGH. S U R R E N D E R. SURRENDER yourself to the Time of the Three D.

The Time of the Three D is the Time of the Woman, the Time of the Goddess, the Time of DIVINITY.

D as Ma*D*onna—Female Physical Expression manifested in a body.

D as Go*D*dess—Divine-Human Creator Deity.

D as Divinity—Expression of the Spirit in the androgynous body.

Breathe, Breathe . . . breathe and listen . . .

I address the circles of Women: the ancient Priestesses who return, the burnt Women transformed into Gold, the raped

Women transformed into Masters, the Women friends, the wayfaring Sisters of rebellious dreams, the Women sisters of Time, the Women of Egypt, the Crusader Women with hard helmets, the Women victims of an Ancient past.

With Gentle Grace I address to You Holy, to You prostituted, to You witch burned at the stake, to You Woman of the circular time, to You Woman companion of the Sun, to You Woman finally UNITED.

To You Woman finally HEALED.

I come to you Sisters, to you friends. Companions who in the name of the Rose unite your hearts. To you sisters who from the Temples of Tien REunite yourselves again today to celebrate yourselves without more tragedies and wounds.

Souls companion . . . Sing LIFE, dance love. Your wound is HEALED. The healed wound of the womb is transformed into a Cosmic Door of love through a UNIQUE Heart.

Your frequency has changed. Manifest it! What are you waiting for?

DIVINITY manifests itself without veils. It manifests itself in the SACRED body. It manifests itself through the New Frequency. It manifests itself through the New Vibration. It manifests itself through the Sound that becomes Word, through the KRISTIC Logos that becomes Form.

Everything is ready. You are ready.

For what? For who?

Enchanting Divine Creatures, UNION has happened within you.

Your Union welcomes you and welcomes the one who was born of You. It welcomes the Masculine with no more revenge, no more anger or resentment. Anger toward the masculine no longer makes sense: Isis's wound is healed, Magdalene's wound is healed. Anger toward the male outside You is the illusion that separates you and distracts you from YOURSELF.

Allow your Sacred Feminine to express herself in her NATURE, and let your DIVINE Masculine allow himself to act in self-confidence and not RE-act in fear of You.

To express your Creative Feminine, give voice to your Divine Masculine and listen to his melody.

A masculine who is ALLOWED to feel, a masculine who is allowed to let go of the need to DEMONSTRATE, a masculine who recognizes the sweetness of his Strength and the Tenderness of his Virility.

Breathe . . . breathe soul companion.

Breathe . . . breathe and listen.

In this Time the frequency of the Three D has anchored in your heart.

From the bowels of Earth the new portal of the Celestial Light opens, where a stream of New water unravels. Crinkled Crystals of New Diamonds.

I Am the Eternal Consciousness of Mary Magdalene, and with Gentle Grace to YOU, I come with a message of Eternal Consciousness. The energy of the New Earthly Vibration, where you WOMAN Master of YOU become Master of the occult secrets, now ready to be revealed.

The wound of the Female womb is healed, and the wound of the HEART of the man is healing. Yes, it is in the heart that man has his wound. Beyond what has manifested itself in the visible over the course of the different eras, the Male Heart has a great wound, and NOW, in the time of the GODDESS, it is ready to transform it.

The PAIN inflicted on the WOMAN is the pain that he himself has exerted on his Creative Power. The Fear of being a CREATOR blocked the flow of his Mastery, and recognizing himself as a false POWER, he raped himself in self-blindness. By raping the Woman, he raped his Mastery, giving voice to the ancestral resentment toward the Feminine being. He raped his innate ability to Create, chasing the memory of the womb, which today he begins to recognize in his heart. To avoid surrendering to his own creative love, he preferred to hate himself and be hated.

Now in the Time of the Three D, everything is ready.

The new MASCULINE with Love falls in love with himself and in love learns to give birth to his MASTERY.

Now, in the NEW TIME it is no longer Time for the Feminine to hold grudges toward those who have been afraid of their own Power. These emotions slow down the expansion of the Body of Consciousness, which instead demands the ardent desire to manifest itself in its true beauty.

This change in frequency in the becoming of the Eternal Consciousness gently allows the Masculine to let go of himself to the manifestation of his own Essence.

All of this will bring about a great Change in Parental Relations.

All of this will bring about a great Change in Couple Relations.

MANY COUPLE RELATIONS WILL FORM IN THE PLEASURE OF BEING WITH THE OTHER AND NOT IN THE FEAR OF THE LACK OF THE OTHER.

This will happen because you will let go of the need for attention, the need for attention on the part of the male. It will happen because the virus of seduction, of manipulation will give way to the pure essence of love that feeds only on itself.

When I urge you to help the Masculine outside You, I am not saying to fall into the OLD ENERGY of the Red Cross nurse or to forgive because you like to hear that you are good or to set yourself up as a TEACHER to the Male. This dynamic is obsolete and is no longer useful for Your expansion. It tastes of revenge; it makes you stay in the old energy. In the Time of Creation you do not need it. Energy must be invested not wasted.

With Gentle Grace I invite you to remain UNITED with YOURSELF.

I invite you to allow Your inner Masculine to soften and Your Feminine to expand in its cup of Creating MOTHER.

United with Yourself you will be able to WELCOME and love the MASCULINE without more pretensions, without more needs, without more judgments, without the need to FEED YOURSELF. Be sensual, not seductive. Sensuality is the Flame of Your Passion, and Passion is the Flame of Life.

I welcome you in the crystalline heart of Earth, luminous souls.

I invite you to have Faith in the New Time.

I speak of Faith, not religion—Faith in the TIME OF CREATION is the Mastery of You, is the awareness that the Divine-Human UNIFIES, and aware of himself, he manifests himself.

In the New Time there is no Krist who descends into a physical body and then dies on a cross. There is no WOMAN who is misunderstood, concealed, and singled out as a PROSTITUTE. There is the androgynous being who Awakens, recognizing himself in the equity of the Kristic Seed and through the Physical Body experiences the Joy and the Passion of HUMAN existence.

I love you deeply, companion souls.

I love you deeply, Divine souls.

I love you deeply, souls of Grace.

IN THE AKASHIC ROOMS

The scent of sandalwood intoxicates us. Incense smoke harmoniously creates eight Circles in the air.

Our KRISTal guided us. We are ready to explore a new *Circular Room*. Shavings of velvety petals imbue the room before our eyes with intense passion. Myrrh powder stored in Golden Grails glistens with new information. Alabaster ampoules spread the intense scent of cedar. Leaves of bay and sage create sovereign Crowns. The balm of the soul is ready to Love us.

The sensuality of the new akashic space evokes in us the game of angels; many of them seem never to have incarnated. They welcome us.

The WONDER of love attracts us, excites us, intrigues us. The angels appear to be all male.

"Male? But . . . but do angels not have sex?" Joy asks with extreme naïveté.

Myriam's burst into a joyful laugh makes the new experience we are about to have joyful.

Myriam laughs heartily. She involves us so much in her joy that we forget the question Joy posed to her.

"It is new for you to see me laugh, right? For years you have looked for me, and for centuries you have painted me sad, suffering, penitent, a VICTIM. That's enough! That's enough!" Myriam rejoices joyfully. "LIFE is JOY! LIFE is JOY!"

Like a Creature with no past or future, Myriam opens her arms and with infinite love emits her sound:

"Life is JOY, life is JOY, life is JOY . . . ," she repeats several times.

Wonderful! We start to like the wonder of wonder. The experience we are about to have in our SPACE is inviting and very attractive.

Myriam is particularly sensual. Her light clothes reveal the softness of her body. She is pure. She is beautiful. She is elegantly simple. Around her neck she wears a very long ivory-colored scarf that contrasts with the dark of her long auburn hair.

She is very smiley. It is as if she is waiting for someone who makes her heart beat. She looks euphoric; no, we soon realize that she is very excited.

Like a woman in love who waits for her Beloved, she waits confidently and certain of his arrival. An immense golden Light dazzles us. The whole Universe is there with us to celebrate the Male Kristic Seed who appears in his New Sovereignty.

The breath becomes silence. The Wonder emits his sound. Beauty, Amazement, and lots of grace. As timeless children we let ourselves be embraced by the warmth of Yeshua who is much more Human than what we expected. Hand in hand, the Eternal Lovers in their Sovereign humanity Give us the presence of their Union.

Myriam and Yeshua . . . What a thrill to see them Together. The heart cannot stop; it beats madly with both a tribal and sacred rhythm.

"Time? But there is no time. Is there only this instant that is called the Eternal Present?" Joy asks in amazement.

Their gaze is indefinable. It is so unique that it is too difficult to shape it with words. Only the heart rhythm can speak. Only the heart rhythm becomes the wedding march of the Human Cosmic Couple.

Their PRESENCE is present.

Their vibration emits the sound of UNION.

Like a young girl in love with her first love, she looks deeply into his eyes. He smiles and in front of such a beauty exults his Joy.

Together, they burst into a loud laugh, embracing each other, hugging each other, while he with the impetus of passion lifts her upward. The air is joyful. Joy overflows and hops among thousands of multicolored butterflies. The human angels party. Rose petals, chopped almonds, grains of rice, the scent of lilies, it is all very contagious.

Myriam and Yeshua smile at life and exult in unison:

"LIFE IS JOY!

LIFE IS NOW!

ENOUGH DRAMA!

ENOUGH PAIN!

ENOUGH PAST!

ENOUGH CROSSES!

ENOUGH STAKES!

ENOUGH!"

The music of the heart is so high that Myriam and Yeshua, without ever getting lost in their gaze, begin to dance, having fun, rejoicing, involving us in the Sacred Spiral of the Cosmic Union.

Myriam looks at Yeshua and with an intriguing smile beckons him, inviting him to take a step forward, just as they do on the stages of the New Energy, where the scenes of the Akashic stories change in honor of the New Time.

He, brilliant and passionate, observes us for a long time, reading in us the amazement of those who expected a Yeshua pierced with blood soaked thorns, his hands showing the indelible marks of the nails of the cross.

"What you expected of me is old. It is ancient, it is obsolete, it is false, it is a fairy tale. In the New Akashic Rooms, there is no memory that remembers. There is PRESENCE that Creates.

There is Eternal Consciousness created by the awakened human. But do you really think that after many centuries I was still here crying desperately for what has been? Or rather for what they made you believe?"

Yeshua looks at Myriam and, taking her hands, kisses her with tender passion and looking into her eyes he says: *"I LOVE YOU, I LOVE YOU, my love."*

Suddenly, the sunshine of Yeshua becomes a strong Presence. His eyes seem like vehicles through which to travel beyond Time, beyond Space. His deep voice becomes ageless. Myriam silently moves away, leaving him his Space without interfering.

"The Time of the Three D, which speaks so much of Woman, is actually the time of the New Masculine."

Yeshua continues.

"In the Time of the Goddess, the masculine allows himself to live his inner feminine and finds his Divine Masculine. The awakened woman, united with herself, invites her heart to return home."

He turns to Myriam and, nodding his head, lovingly admires her, indicating her as an example.

"Two thousand years ago, my human body suffered a lot, but I was not afraid of what was happening. My death was not your fault, which they made you believe for centuries.

How many times as a child under the cross have they told you:

'Look, he died because of you!' And You in your silent innocence asked yourself: 'But I did not do anything.'

You could not oppose it yourself: it was so. Someone had decided it. In reality, however, something did not resonate in your heart though, did it?

That ancient sense of guilt was woven into the human skin, and like a thorn it stuck in the hearts of men and in the wombs of women. By subconsciously blaming yourself for a wrongdoing that you never committed, you have attracted many experiences to You through which to punish yourself. As you became convinced of that falsehood, you have created the conviction in You: 'I do not deserve it! I am not worthy!'

The sense of guilt acted in silence by deluding you into believing that its source lay in the traumatic events of your childhood, which you could discover through studying the psyche. Yes, of course, examining the pysche and your childhood is also useful, but the sense of guilt is more than two thousand years old, much older than your personal history.

In the becoming of your existences, you have changed vessels

many times, but the perception of the sense of guilt, kept in the memory, has followed you in every life.

NOW, through the awareness of who you are, this memory imbued with you returns to its Origin.

BREATHE, soul companion. Breathe.

Breathe and know that You are not at fault.

You are INNOCENT!

You are INNOCENT!

You are INNOCENT!

Forgive yourself, forgive yourself for having believed to be guilty.

Take a deep breath. FREE YOURSELF from that old Consciousness. Breathe even more deeply and let the New Energy enter YOU.

My journey was mine, Yours is Yours, so everyone has his own responsibility.

Why should I take charge of Your problems and You of mine if in both of us flows Royal Blood? Why?

I love You deeply. I support you. I have always done so, but I cannot choose for You.

The choice is Yours! The journey is Yours!

In the New Time we are CREATORS, not spectators.

We are MASTERS, not adepts."

Yeshua turns to look at Myriam. He is enchanted by her beauty, and as he looks at her, he says, *"With Magdalene . . ."*

He remains in silence. He remains in silence for a few moments entranced by the Sweet Firmness that Myriam emanates and then continues to speak, indicating her with his left hand.

"With her we taught about love and the union of the two forces inherent in the human: the Masculine and the Feminine. My long journey that they never told you about helped me find the SPIRIT I had been looking for so much. It helped me to discover that God-Goddess harbored within ME.

I owe a lot to MY MOTHER who left me free to live my journey without ever hindering the path of my soul. On the physical plane I was a son, and she was a mother. She could have done it, but she did not because SHE was a great WOMAN. A wise MASTER who welcomed my body in her womb. She is beautiful Mary, isn't she? My Mother."

Yeshua smiles in all his splendor, unleashing a deep emotion.

"I am very grateful to Myriam who has preserved the secrets of love to be able to propagate them after two thousand years in the Time of Creation. SHE, aware of the intense experiences that would have awaited her in her various lives, was able to wait in TRUST for her own return. What you have been told about me is very different from my real story. Some papyri have been lost; others are still closed. Others have been found, but are still kept in powerful chests . . . "

He looks at Myriam. He winks at her with a deep understanding and complicity.

"In all these centuries, from my death to NOW, they have given birth to me every year. Every year they made me resur-

rect. *Repeated and perpetuated images of pain, drama, lack, and suffering. These were the looms on which the human has forcibly woven his unreal story. I knew that it would have taken another two millennia before humanity awakened, and this would have happened in the Time of Awakening thanks to . . ."*

Yeshua turns to his Beloved and, bowing, continues:

"Thanks to HER and her Frequency.

SHE, Mary Magdalene, does not represent only the woman in the physical sense.

SHE is the Divine Feminine that was torn from the human two thousand years ago.

SHE was missed by everyone.

Men have looked for her in every Woman, and women have looked for ME in every man.

SHE is the Origin.

I do not just represent the Male Kristic Seed. The false story of me has altered the vision of the masculine aspect in the human. Men in the physical sense, seeing in me only the Divine and not the Human Man that I have been, have never allowed themselves to be Divine in their own Body.

So what happened?

What did the confusion between Masculine and Feminine create?

What information did Myriam's false story convey?

What did her absence create?

What did the false story of ME imbue human consciousness with?

I will answer you with simple words.

Yes, simple, because SIMPLE is the Time of Now.

The imbalance between Masculine and Feminine has created the Energy of the nonlove of oneself. The duality between Masculine and Feminine has given way to the separation of the two identities, projecting them out of oneself, thus forgetting the ORIGIN, which is ONE.

The Energy is ONE. The two forces, the two aspects, Masculine and Feminine are the means through which the energy moves. By hiding Myriam from my side, the emptiness in both men and women was immense because both of them deprived themselves of feeling, they deprived themselves of creating, they deprived themselves of welcoming themselves, they deprived themselves of respecting themselves.

The woman often identified herself in what she was not, forgetting the Creative Force of her ovaries, the sacred place in the woman's body where Life is created.

Man looked for Myriam on the outside, thus looking for that intuitive, creative, loving, and sensual part. And when I speak of sensuality, I speak of SENSES, not of sex.

The Lack of my beloved and the false story of me not only led you to seek outside what was inside You, but it deeply ALTERED and HURT the Masculine part of YOU. The Masculine Consciousness, which is in both sexes, has woven itself into a subtle belief that I now wish to speak to you about.

It is about DEFEAT."

"Defeat? But Yeshua, which defeat are you talking about?" Joy asks, more and more amazed.

"Defeat and the fear of FAILURE are the stinging thorn with which the masculine is hurt. To mask pain, man in the physical sense and the masculine as an aspect of the human have Re-acted instead of Acted."

"Yeshua . . . but what do you mean by DEFEAT? Explain to us better," asks Joy.

"Many are the humans who, because of what they have been led to believe, have experienced my death as a DEFEAT. This solidified, turning into insecurity, and became rationality, reaction, control. The need to demonstrate has become the PRIMARY NEED of the human, the Need to Be RECOGNIZED.

Do you understand now why so many women have competed with other women?

Do you understand now why so many women have competed with other men?

Do you understand why so many men have competed with other men?

Between them, it is not about gender diversity, it is about RECOGNITION, the recognition of the Sacred Masculine Strength that allows the Feminine one to express itself.

When strength is SACRED, there is no need to demonstrate.

Without the fear of failure, the masculine part relaxes, stops competing, lets go, and allies with its Feminine Strength.

Here, the androgyny, that is the Cosmic Union, takes shape in its own CUP, in the man's heart and the woman's womb.

Here is where the union happens within You.

I have never failed. I WON MYSELF.

Myriam won herself in every life and now returns to bring the frequency of UNION to Earth. Your silent soul has continued to speak to you of the truth, and You have continued to seek it in every existence. SHE feels a deep love and a great JOY for You when you TRUST YOURSELF, when you let yourself go into the healthy awareness that your coming to Earth is recognizing and Enjoying Your Union of Human and Divine. You are one, and you are the other.

Enough with SEPARATION.

ENOUGH with the DRAMA.

Now it is about being GRATEFUL for everything that has happened, grateful for all the experiences you have had; it is about celebrating because thanks to the false story of ME, to the altered story of Magdalene and You, you have never stopped LOOKING FOR YOURSELF.

As I made my journey then, You did Yours.

NOW you ARE here. Rejoice, you are here. You got here.

Yes, here you are in the Time of the Eternal Consciousness.

CONGRATULATE yourself.

Celebrate yourself. Honor yourself. THANK YOURSELF.

YOU ARE FREE.

FREE from the fear of failing.

FREE from the fear of demonstrating.

FREE from the fear of being judged.
FREE from the fear of not being WORTHY.
FREE from the fear of death."

Yeshua turns right and realizes that MAGDALENE is there with folded hands, thanking him. Yeshua pulls her to him and passionately kisses her on the mouth. A human kiss, deep, intense, and between one breath and another, he whispers to her:

"I have always continued to kiss you. From then until now I have never stopped."

He holds her even tighter to him.

Breathe . . . allow yourself to Breathe, allow yourself to feel UNITED.

Now, here in this instant without judgment and complete with YOU, carry Myriam and Yeshua United by Your love in your heart. Breathe into your heart the Human PASSION of Yeshua and Myriam and observe how much FREEDOM and space this union has created within you. Feel the COMPLETENESS within you. Allow yourself to INTEGRATE every ASPECT of You and observe the love You Are . . .

THERE . . . that is the love you have always been looking for.

In the name of the Rose, so it is.

11

In the Apparent World

I welcome you soul companions in my heart.

I welcome and LOVE you deeply.

Bring who you ARE to the world and Enjoy YOU without being DISTRACTED.

In the "apparent" world many are those who let themselves be frightened by the chaos, the crisis, the change that involves every cell and therefore everybody. By the change that involves every person, every blade of grass, every tree, every sea, every climate, every season.

The Energy of the new Seasons breaks the mental schemes of those who do not understand, because Summer becomes cold and Winter becomes hot. The breaking of patterns scares the linear mind. Like an earthquake the new Energy breaks up the old, turning it into rubble; through tsunamis and volcanoes, through apparently "harmful" catastrophes, it shatters the old Energy.

Many are those who are still sleeping and close their eyes to

the life of their SOUL. Many are those who, still VICTIMS, remain in the energies of abuse. Many are those who remain in the old Energy of Me.

In the fabric of the Eternal CONSCIOUSNESS, there is the Energy of TRANSFORMATION that lives in the Present. In the fabric of the Eternal Consciousness that You yourself have created, there is the Eternal Consciousness of Me.

What does "Eternal Consciousness of Me" mean?

MYRIAM, MARY MAGDALENE, MARY of MAGDALA are all names that have been given to my person, to my life, to my story, to my earthly story with Yeshua. Now, in the New Time, I Return to tell you to Live me, not to remember me. I come back to breathe in You, not to be looked for in old papyri. Live me, this is it. Live You, this is it.

When you transform Conflict into Awareness, you become the diamond alchemist who TRANSFORMS your life into a New Creation. You become the Master of the Temples who already KNOWS.

When you enter within Yourself without letting yourself be DISTRACTED, You transform what hurts you into what makes you live.

TRANSFORMATION, this I AM.

The Origin, this I Am!

My story with Yeshua is real and authentic; it existed and exists. Soon, without effort and without too much research, the truth will come out. Do not force yourself to prove, do not force yourself to prove my presence in those Times. I live in You NOW!

Now, in this instant, as you breathe.

Union and Transformation, this I AM!

Every time You feel United with Yourself, YOU live me.

I AM You every time you CHOOSE Yourself.

I AM You every time you LOVE Yourself.

I AM You every time You are the Creator of your own life!

Master, by staying in the old Energy of Me you remain among the dormants who still believe that the crisis is economic or political and that the fault is always someone's: the state, the mother, the husband, destiny, a divine punishment. The only real crisis of the Divine-Human is that of the SPIRIT.

When I speak of SPIRIT, I do not speak of religion. I speak of the recognition of You as Spirit on Earth.

I speak of the recognition of Your MASTERY.

I speak of the recognition of Your Royal Blood.

I speak of the recognition of Your Divine DNA.

I speak of the recognition of Your Sacred Feminine, of the CREATIVE Power that is in the womb of Your heart, whether YOU are a man or YOU are a woman.

Do not be DISTRACTED by sexual difference.

The CREATIVE Power is inherent in Your Androgynous Being. When you are in Your HEART and you love Yourself deeply, you become Aware that no CRISIS can ever DISTRACT from YOURSELF.

The distraction is the nourishment of the ego.

The distraction is the forgetfulness of the MASTERY.

The distraction is the lack of YOU.

The distraction is the lack of Responsibility of your own life.

If you lack Yourself, you are ABSENT. The distraction takes over by feeding on You.

When you are in your MASTERY, you are PRESENCE, and in the PRESENCE of You, there is NOTHING you can miss.

The attention to the other as the cause of what you live is DISTRACTION.

NO ONE CAN BE WITH THE OTHER IF HE LACKS HIMSELF.

NO ONE CAN BE WITH THE OTHER IF SHE LACKS HERSELF.

The attention to the symptom as the cause of your discomfort is DISTRACTION.

The observation of You, the action for you, the absence of judgment of You, and the awareness of who you ARE, this is PRESENCE, this is MASTERY!

The attention to Yourself as the DIVINE-HUMAN CREATOR of your life is LIFE!

NOW stop, breathe, breathe . . . Breathe and listen . . .

With Gentle Grace allow yourself to BREATHE, breathe and take for Yourself, breathe and let the ETERNAL CONSCIOUSNESS of Me enter into You.

Do nothing, just breathe!

BREATHE, let the New Energy into You. TRUST.

In the time of Creation, many are the awakened ones who have chosen JOY. Many others, however, are still in the

density of their visible bodies and are part of the dormants.

Let go without holding back those who have made their CHOICE.

Even if it is someone you LOVE deeply, LET HIM GO.

It can be a SON, a LOVER, a MOTHER, a FRIEND . . . let him go.

Let him go.

Your journey is not His . . . and His journey is not Yours.

Everyone follows the directives of his SOUL and his JOURNEY. Everyone RESPECTS the rhythm of his journey, and in respect of it he MEETS with his soul.

The evolutionary JOURNEY goes beyond any ROLE.

The soul is neither Father nor Mother, neither wife nor husband, neither friend nor enemy. The soul does not compete. She does not win; she does not reach any goal. She does not feed on faults or merits. Neither applause nor booing. She does not judge, she does not manipulate, she does not wait. She lives. She simply LIVES.

TO LIVE, ONLY THIS THERE IS.

Through the body, the soul just wants to LIVE its experience on the water planet. This is.

In the NEW you need nothing but your PRESENCE.

Do not try too hard to understand how the NEW Time works.

In the NEW everything happens without too much understanding.

Do not make too many PROGRAMS. These, if they are

not in line with the directives of your soul, crumble through sometimes painful experiences.

Do not create too many GOALS: the New Energy shatters them.

CHOOSE. Choice is different from decision. The first comes from the creative womb; the second comes from the mind. The choice arises from the INTENT to open yourself to the flow of your life without judging it, by learning to OBSERVE IT.

Allow yourself to FREE YOURSELF from what is DISTRACTING you. Think with your heart and create with your soul. Experience your MULTIDIMENSIONAL being.

Your journey to other worlds brings you valuable information. It leads you to remember who you Are. Remain receptive and without too much understanding remember and TRUST! Very often your SELF is engaged in other worlds and realities, seeing and knowing things that you cannot see yet because your mind wants to understand.

You will see . . . soon many discoveries will come to you. These will not be the discoveries of science, which dictates laws. No, they will be the discoveries you will make on the journey of the Divine-Human on Earth and therefore on YOURSELF.

Soon many children will tell you ancient truths: LISTEN to THEM. Let them TALK. Follow their INSTRUCTIONS. Avalanches of MASTERS have descended on the planet, and you will soon recognize them. They know very well the power *of the thinking heart, and this, compared to the power of the mind, is nothing.*

Breathe . . . breathe and listen . . .

Yeshua and I are two sides of the same coin. Let go of our physicality. Let go of our story. Feel us in our FREQUENCY. If you can perceive it, you will feel that it is the same frequency You RADIATE when you LOVE Yourself deeply, when you Unite every part of You.

Soul companion, know that all is done.

REST. RELAX. REJOICE.

The Dance has just begun.

YOU ARE THE ALL, AND YOU EXIST IN THE ALL.

IN THE AKASHIC ROOMS

In the expansion of New Energy we really start to have fun; the KRISTal companion of our journey guides us by indicating the New *Circular Room* to explore.

A chant-like sound is heard coming from the center of the new space. *Crea-ti-vity, Crea-ti-vity* . . . It seems an ancient song, but present. What was suddenly becomes What IS. Intrigued, we wonder where the sensual and angelic voice comes from. No clue. Without understanding too much, as it is natural in the New Energy, Joyful like children we open ourselves to the new.

We breathe deeply, allowing the New Energy to flow

into us, as the chanting from afar continues to echo:

C r e a . . . t i . . . v i t y y y y y y y y y . . .

The strong echo resonates perfectly in the center of each of our cells, and our DNA begins to dance, awakening ancient memories: Atlantis, Lemuria, and even before . . . the Whole.

THE ORIGIN.

THE MATER.

The sensuality of the new SPACE intrigues us; the celestial echo of C R E A T I V I T Y gradually frees our layers enabling everything to emerge in the form of memory.

"Layers? But which layers?" Joy does not have time to ask himself the questions that his consciousness answers. Our vision is captivated by what the mind is not programmed to understand. We are enchanted. Colors in a thousand shades flutter lightly, like light refracted through diamonds. Lost, sovereign Crowns capture our desire to experience. We let ourselves be completely involved in the BEYOND.

"Beyond? Beyond where? What is this space? But . . . mmm . . . but where are we?" Joy asks, bewildered.

"It is the Circular Room of the twelve," Myriam replies, appearing in a soft and light dress: colors ranging from soft pink to strong purple, from celestial blue to intense blue. A royal golden crown illuminates the oval of her face.

Myriam is so Beautiful that she seems sculpted by the New Leonardo.

"New Leonardo? Room of the Twelve? Crowns? Go

Beyond? . . . I do not understand anything anymore in this New Energy!" Joy states smiling and clearly feeling that something in him is changing.

Myriam, happy, continues to laugh out loud, starting to emit the SOUND of our names. What a wonderful feeling to be called by our name through sound. An expansive energy clears the images and memories of past experiences.

Myriam, embellished by the Sovereignty of her CROWN, invites us to observe the CENTER from which the chant comes and in which the GOLDEN ARMCHAIR is placed. Each one of us is curious, and she, with refined Mastery, invites us to sit on the regal golden yellow armchair, which seems to have been waiting for us since the time of the origin.

As soon as we sit, our Consciousness moves into the King and the Queen's room. Immersed in the Royalty of the colors of GOLD, we are given *symbols* and *keys* to access other places. Everything is fast, and in the sudden following breath, we are already in other spaces.

A strong emotion suddenly blocks our breath; the eyes of our soul begin to SEE clearly. An unparalleled scenery is visible to our eyes.

Before us the Fathers of all our infinite existences, the Mothers of all our infinite lives, the MOTHER and FATHER of all our experiences, including the last of this life.

The King and Queen in the background observe compassionately.

How many lives, how many experiences, how many ASPECTS are all there, in front of us. Each existence was different, sometimes man, others woman. Sometimes victim, others executioner. Nun, priest, perhaps pope or pharaoh, king and even warrior. Sometimes poor, others rich. Each time with a different aspect, each life in a different place.

Breathe soul companion. Breathe and listen . . .

"You, who in the New Time of Awakening, have been everywhere. You know well the planet on which you have chosen to BE. So many of you have incarnated many times in France, in Palestine, in the Middle East, and in all those places where we met. I do not mean with Yeshua, but with You, with You listening in this moment.

Breathe . . .

NOW FINALLY YOU ARE HERE. Here in the Time of Awakening. I know it was not easy for you to get here, but finally you are here, you HAVE arrived. You did it!

The Eternal Consciousness is NOW.

Now become aware that the Roles, the aspects of Your different experiences, have always been different. You have not always been a Mother in all your lives, you have not always been a Father, but there is an experience you have always had, that of being a SON or a DAUGHTER. That one, yes, you have always lived!

In every life you had a Mother and in every life you had a Father that perhaps in some existences you have not even known. It does not matter. No matter how it went, you have always been

a son or a daughter born of a FATHER and a MOTHER who deep inside You reminded you of the Parents of the Spirit. They reminded you of that place That Was. The Whole. The origin. They reminded you of the HOME You left.

Now, in the Divine moment of the Present, the eyes of your soul see the blurred faces of all the Parents who have been part of your infinite experiences.

What a deep emotion it is, isn't it?

How many memories. How many emotions.

In every life you have lived through your Parents, some wonderful experiences, others very painful.

You believed in their models and you reacted to them by completely deviating, or you repurposed them by imitating their own script. In every life you have carried the perspective of the Parenting patterns received in the previous life, and forgetting who YOU ARE, you have never allowed yourself to Enjoy the wonderful experience of Being a Divine-Human."

"The twelve? The Whole? Home?" Joy asks with more and more interest.

"Twelve are the layers in which the TREASURE in the origin was kept. You have looked for it everywhere and in anyone. Science made you believe that it did not exist, and religion tried to keep it on concrete altars. Only NOW you are discovering that it was so close to you. Only NOW you are becoming Aware."

Lightly, we let ourselves flow through the new information. We Create the Void, and let it, with experience, become imbued with New Awareness.

"When you were just an angel, you were asked: 'Who wants to descend?' You immediately raised a finger up in a sign of victory: 'I' you affirmed enthusiastically. In reality, you still did not know if it really was victory.

With love you made Your choice, but immediately afterward, you were very afraid because in a single moment you saw all your existences and what awaited you. You immediately changed your mind. You wanted to go home, but you did not know how to go back. That was how you found yourself in the Void, that VOID that you have experienced so many times and that often has frightened you. You started wandering. You felt loneliness, guilt, and even anger together with fear. You wandered, fighting here and there with some angel you met, begging from him for a little Light to feed you, believing that this would help you go home. You forgot to have with You the treasure kept in your precious helices, and you went down headlong into MATTER, forgetting everything."

"Everything? All what?" Joy asks with eyes filled with amazement.

"You forgot you were DIVINE. You forgot the story of the Spirit, the story of the origin, the story of consciousness."

"Origin? Consciousness? So what happened?" Joy goes on, more and more eager to know.

"It happened that the SPIRIT wondered: 'Who Am I?'

To see himself he created You. He mirrored himself in YOU and fell madly in love with YOU. The parents of the Spirit—the King and Queen, your Masculine and Feminine—loved each other to such an extent that they are always one THING within You.

You forgot this. Thus it was that in Atlantis you separated yourself.

Life after life, experience after experience. NOW you have arrived here. Here, where the Circle finally ends.

Here, SPACE where you become aware that all the entities that have been part of your previous existences return home together with the soul garments that accompanied you in this last existence. Here, NOW, it remains only what you are, your DIVINITY in physical form Enjoying the beauty of life.

GOD is the sound used to indicate GOD, and GOD's only desire is that You ENJOY the beauty of life. It is that you understand that at the origin there was no separation, but to understand this, for countless times, you have experienced separation.

NOW dance if you want to dance, paint if you want to paint, sing if you want to sing. This is the expression of crea-ti-vity.

Whenever you breathe You are Spirit in Matter.

This is the Spirit of the Living Creator."

The awareness of what is happening brings us back to the Here and Now.

Festive Crystal children greet us. One of them, particularly charming, has a very particular brush in his hand and a palette of New Colors that the linear mind cannot define. On his face is the complicit smile of a woman, like that of the Mona Lisa.

Could it be Leonardo who returned happy to be able to tell everyone the truth he already knew then?

With no more drama, pain, and suffering, the New and Sensual painting of Yeshua and Myriam is ready.

NOW their love is finally FREE.

FREE like YOU, as you listen and remember who You Are.

NOW YOU KNOW. NOW YOU ARE.

I choose to let go of all painful experiences toward the energy of the MASCULINE that I have lived in the different existences in me and outside of me. I choose NOW to TRANSFORM THEM into Support, Trust, and Love.

I choose to let go of all painful experiences toward the energy of the FEMININE that I have lived in the different existences in me and outside of me. I choose NOW to TRANSFORM THEM into Acceptance, Love, and Intuition.

I thank all the Mothers and Fathers of my various existences.

With deep love I thank the MOTHER and FATHER for this present existence. They were the means by which to return to ME. They were the means by which to return to the Mother and Father that I Am today.

Father and Mother of me . . . I CREATE MY LIFE.

In the name of the Rose, so it is.

12

Games
and Symbolisms

*I*n the heart of Silence I introduce myself to You.

In the heart of love I come to YOU.

From the heart of the New Era I speak to You.

The PARADIGMS change and the protagonists wear New clothes.

Light clothes, Transparent clothes, Versatile clothes.

Everything changes in the becoming of every moment, and the human, even the dormant one, acquires awareness.

What happens? What is happening?

It happens that the awakened Enjoy the New Time without letting themselves be influenced by the obsolete past. They have stopped looking for answers. They live, Enjoy being Present, and like a beacon they RADIATE Eternal Consciousness.

They are those who ARE without doing anymore, who

ARE without saying anymore, who ARE without convincing anymore, who ARE without Fighting anymore.

Their frequency becomes MAGNETIC, and like a tuning fork they awaken the harmony of the New Human History in the other.

The dormants, on the other hand, in their Spiritual Spring, slowly begin to open their eyes, letting the first Ray of the New Energy enter within them. Many of them do not understand, many are frightened, many are passionate, many are curious, and many others, instead, begin to open up to the frequency of the Eternal Consciousness.

Everything changes while the newborn Alchemist-Human lives New Experiences.

The game of drama and suffering as an experience of Earthly life, for those who have CHOSEN the NEW, begins to become an increasingly faded black-and-white photo. It convinces less and less even those who, still on their knees far from themselves, hope and pray, believing that the help comes from Outside.

Divine Soul, with Gentle Grace I come to You and with Sweet Firmness I speak to You . . .

The Time in which you will see me on the altars next to my beloved is getting closer and closer. Soon the JOY of my smile will awaken the heart of *"the one who dressed in white"* and will bring overwhelming changes that have never happened before in human history. New discoveries will speak of the twenty-two caves of Crystal in line with the twenty-two portals distributed on the WATER PLANET.

These connect the Spiritual world to the Physical one, and through the different *Rays* will awaken the Ancestral Divine Energy of every place and every human being. On many Sacred Lands, religious temples have been built. Cults and different information have imbued these lands, altering them with respect to their ORIGIN. The underlying energy of the different Portals is Sacred, not religious. SPIRITUAL energy is beyond any CREED.

Religions, groups, different cults separate. SPIRIT Unites.

And it is precisely in the UNION that humanity will experience a great change.

How will this happen?

It will happen effortlessly, through the New Frequency, thanks to which even science will surrender to the invisible. Science will begin to whisper that perhaps it was wrong on many things and with great caution will disclose the New Discoveries, using the merit of research.

At first it will be just a whisper; later, it will be a real hymn to the new paradigm.

It also happened in me.

"Someone" whispered that they were wrong about Mary Magdalene: the penitent was not a prostitute.

Of course, they did not add that I was Yeshua's beloved, but have FAITH, soon this too will happen, and the great MASS will know. It will be then that the human will allow himself to feel completely the Feminine part of himself.

The New Frequency cannot be buried; it has already been done and that time is over. The seed of silence has grown in the womb of the Mother Goddess, and in her natural Grace, NOW Gives birth to the Truth of Human existence.

The truth always comes out. It is a universal law that the linear human mind can no longer control or manipulate.

Have FAITH.

I did not say to believe in a doctrine. I said have FAITH; it is different.

Through the frequency of New Codes, the old Information will transform into New beliefs, New thoughts, and New discoveries. These will be in tune with the frequency of the Sun. The KRISTIC solar Energy opens the door of life. This door is the Pineal Gland; it connects you directly to the center of your Soul.

The sun is the Tao of the Universe. It contains the King and Queen within, the masculine who gives and the feminine who receives.

The sun is the Energy of the Kristic Gold through which the human can transform coal into Gold, old beliefs into new Information, ignorance into Awareness, knowledge into Consciousness. Just as the seed needs the sun to become flower and then fruit, so the human needs the solar Kristic Energy to become Aware and then CONSCIOUS.

Breathe soul companion . . . breathe and listen.

Every problem you experience is the result of earthly information you have received, but it has nothing to do with Your Kristic Soul.

You are OTHER. You are BEYOND!

Whenever you experience what You believe to be a problem, go BEYOND and ask yourself:

"Besides being a Man who am I?"

"Besides being a Woman who am I?"

"Besides being a Mother, who am I?"

"Besides being a Father, who am I?"

"Besides being what I do, what I know, and what I have, who AM I?"

YOU ARE. This is the point! You are pure consciousness.

THE I AM without contours is the CENTER!

In the I AM the problem dissolves.

In the I AM you allow yourself to exist.

Step into the ray of your SOUL and Radiate what YOU ARE.

Magnetism does not depend on knowledge.

MAGNETISM DEPENDS ON THE CHARISMA OF YOUR SOUL.

You Are What You Are, not what you know. In Your being there is already the ancestral knowledge of NEW CODES. You just need to remember.

And as you gain awareness . . . you remember.

You do not need to CHANGE. You just need to become aware of who You Are.

If you are suffering from a physical discomfort, you do not need to HEAL; you need to Connect. It is different.

MASTERY is Transformation, not healing.

COMPLETENESS is Union, not healing.

If you continue to speak about healing, there is still old energy inside You. There is old information that makes you believe in the disease, which leads you to need external tools, which leads you to look for answers outside. SURRENDER. The external tool works because within you You have CHOSEN to return to You, because you have truly CHOSEN to Love You.

LOVING YOURSELF is not a concept. LOVING YOURSELF is an Experience.

Exploring yourself is the practice of Experience transformed into Awareness. It is not enough to read and know; it is not enough to praise what you read if it remains only a reading. Knowledge does not lie in what others have lived, even if it is the great Masters who made the History of humanity and THANKS to which many aspects of humans have evolved. That is their history, not YOURS.

That is why I ask you not to look for the smallest details in my story: that is your mind that wants to know. Your soul does not care much; your soul wants to LIVE its journey through YOU.

In the New Time it is no longer Time to know the past History. It is Time to live the Present life.

Breathe soul companion . . . breathe and listen.

New Schools will be born. The CHILDREN, who are also the Masters of the New Humanity, will study in the woods. They will sit next to a blossoming flower to understand its life. They will not study anatomy in books. They will live their experiences through Purity and Innocence.

In the school of New Energy, the subjects will no longer be history and geography. The new subjects will be Awareness, Play, Silence, Joy, and Love. There will be no competition in getting one vote higher than the other. The vote of MASTERY is the same for everyone, and the children of Eternal Consciousness already know this.

The Parents of old energy will awaken thanks to them. A few of them will not do so right away; a few of them will need more time and more lives. But for all there will be the Awakening, and everyone will vibrate with new frequencies.

MASTERY does not deny anything of what has been.

MASTERY is the feminine part of the human that allows itself to feel by letting go of "understanding." There is no struggle between understanding and feeling. There is no winner or loser. There is an openness to what has remained silent for too long in the feminine hemisphere.

What had Value should not be criticized or judged. It was the experience that the Divine-Human needed to arrive here in the most beautiful moment of human existence. Believe in this: this is the most expanded moment that humanity has ever been able to experience.

Let it flow, life is like water, let it flow.

YOU are the seed planted in the womb of the Mother that goes Beyond my presence on Earth.

MOTHER GODDESS was born with the Origin of Creation.

When I arrived in the Land of Magdala, I carried a lot of past with me, and there are many experiences that I lived in my subsequent lives. My soul, in the bodies of different Women and Men, has lived other stories, stamping the history of humanity with fire. Like You, in every life, I have changed my body. I have lived strong and different experiences, but it is only through the light kept in my eyes that my Origin has manifested itself.

Love yourself, Divine Soul, love yourself and be aware of who YOU ARE.

You are the Origin from which the verb became a word.

YOU are MASTER of your Universal Life.

Universal in the land dear to me is pronounced "Uni-vers-elle":

UNITED TOWARD HER.

Uni-Vers-Elle . . . United Toward HER . . . But who is SHE?

SHE, infused with my Frequency, is your SOUL.

IN THE AKASHIC ROOMS

Myriam appears in the light of her Kristic color. This time she is completely NAKED.

No dress covers her, no aspect of her prevents us from looking at her into the depths of the soul.

She is charismatic, radiant. Her infinitely transparent eyes attract some, at times frighten others. Someone finds an excuse . . . he gets distracted from himself and disappears.

Joy breathes without being DISTRACTED by anything or anyone.

He is there, curious, amazed. He breathes deeply and knows that no one will be able to stop him. He observes without judging despite the embarrassment of the GODDESS's nudity.

Next to Myriam is Yeshua. He too is naked; no tunic covers his body. Only his golden light embodies his vessel, only the scent of his skin is now felt, only his voice is now heard.

"Who is SHE?" reiterates Yeshua.

"She is my beloved, the woman I have loved deeply. Although before her I had a painful experience with a young woman, thanks to whom my search began. I was only a kid when I met her in my Essene school. I fell in love with her like a normal teenager, and soon we let ourselves go into a love relationship. In the strict Essene school that I attended, this was forbidden, which is why we were thrown out. I decided that I would marry that girl, but she died shortly after.

It was then that my dark night of the soul began. Expelled from a school in which I believed blindly, saddened by the loss

of a woman dear to me, imbued with loneliness and in search of my SPIRIT.

Now, as you listen, I feel deep Love and Compassion for You.

I know how many times YOU have felt the same way too. How many times You felt alone without that woman you loved, how many times You felt alone without that man you thought you would marry one day, without that job you believed to be the source of Your economic wealth. How many times have you thought you were at the end? But in reality it is right at that moment that the search for YOU really began. Just like it happened to me. That was when my journey began."

With the firmness and sweetness of one who fears no competition, Myriam, complete of herself, approaches Yeshua, takes the face of her beloved in her hands, looks at him for a long time into the soul of his dark eyes, and gently kisses him on his soft lips.

Yeshua silently begins to cry with Joy on Myriam's chest, feeling the Cup of her welcome.

"But who is SHE?" Joy timidly asks, involved in the physical humanity of Yeshua.

"SHE is not just MY BELOVED MARY MAGDALENE. She is the feminine force that is within YOU. She is the Creation. She is the Sensibility. She is the GRACE. She is the ORIGIN."

Joy has now overcome any fear. He approaches Myriam

amicably as one does with a dear friend, and this time, he does so with the courage of someone who has learned to Look into the eyes. He asks her:

"I want to ask you a question."

"Ask me," Myriam, with Gentle Grace replies.

"You have talked of Grace many times, but what do you mean by 'Grace'?"

Myriam smiles, approaches Joy, takes his hands, and brings them to his heart. She welcomes his gaze without fear, welcomes his gaze full of his PRESENCE. Joy's breathing slows down, creating a rhythmic movement. A perfect wave. His soul floats in his body, feeling completely comfortable. Feeling completely NAKED, Joy undresses himself of every garment and of what is no longer useful to him.

No need. No fear.

Only a deep Connection with his soul.

The breath meanwhile dances the Eternal Consciousness of him.

"That is what GRACE is. Being in deep Intimacy with Yourself. Being connected to YOU. This is GRACE. In the prayers, with which you have been indoctrinated, you often say the WORD GRACE. Being in God's Grace means being CONNECTED to your soul, aware of being GOD.

Allowing your SPIRIT to breathe in You. This is being in a state of GRACE. GRACE is not what you always believed in. It is not the external help that saves you from sin and death, also because you cannot be SAVED from a SIN you

have never committed and from a death that is only an illusion. You Are Eternal. No judge can give you GRACE when YOU are the one putting your SOUL in prison.

Free yourself from the shackles of old beliefs that convinced you that you are what You Are not and live FREE in the GRACE You CREATED.

GRACE is the state of Consciousness where you do not worry about what can happen. It is the sweet trust that comes from the heart, not from the mind. It is allowing your PRESENCE to flow. GRACE is thanking yourself with love for what YOU ARE and for what you have done to get here, here in this time that will one day be spoken of as the TIME OF CREATION, and You who now listen are among the first CREATORS."

Breathe . . . breathe.

Joy feels the lightness of his body, dances in his own belly. He is full of GRACE. He opens his eyes again, and in those of Myriam and Yeshua he mirrors himself. For the first time, he recognizes the same frequency. The look becomes poetry, music, art. The art of making love. No separation, with HER he feels an inseparable flow, sees his ancient soul, remembers the ancient pact, smiles complicity as one who knows that his Creation was perfect. He looks at himself in the eyes of LOVE and recognizes himself there.

Sounds, lights, music, colors, everything seems to be in celebration.

Beams of light caress us. Clear figures of Angels are

transformed into very special children: the Masters of the New Time. Their bright eyes illuminate each of our cells, which meanwhile continue to Transform. The secret of the DNA is in their hands. Genetically different, they will create in different ways, revealing the secret of humanity to the Divine-Human.

Joy NOW knows he is one of them. He surrenders and with them begins the GAME by making dormants believe that he is a human. Complicit in his SPIRIT he lets himself go with Myriam and Yeshua in a deep embrace. He remembers the King and the Queen, he remembers the ALL, he remembers the Promise. NOW he knows he has arrived. NOW he knows that he just has to ENJOY his enlightenment on the planet, to ENJOY the ascension and RADIATE it.

Joy is in a deep state of GRACE.

The Grace that he was able to CREATE himself.

Joy NOW knows that he is truly a SPECIAL being and that everything he has lived through in all his infinite existences has been a useful experience, leading him to arrive now at the Time of Creation and UNITE every part of himself.

Just like it happened to YOU!

In the name of the Rose, so it is.

13

To Create Is to Enjoy

*W*ith Gentle Grace and Sweet Firmness I come to You.

With the Consciousness of the GIFT I speak to You.

Breathe . . . breathe and ask yourself:

What is a Gift for me?

Which frequency has this word for me?

Each word holds the infinite, each word is a sound, each word vibrates with its own music.

Each word has its refrain in its melody.

Gift, GIVE YOURSELF, Give.

Breathe, stop understanding, breathe simply, stay in the flow, stay in what happens without understanding.

Enter inside, allow yourself to enter that part of You that, out of fear, has so often remained outside the door of Home, that is, outside of You because You are Home. Stay here, NOW. Do not search, do not understand, do not analyze. Let the energy come to You. Let yourself be served.

Allow and Trust, simply TRUST.

Breathe and let it happen.

Breath is Creation, and my invitation in this new message is to take you into the Eternal Consciousness of the GIFT, what you do to Yourself when you stop Doing and with an Eternal Consciousness start Creating.

Soul companion . . .

CREATION COMES FROM PLEASURE, NOT FROM EFFORT.

TO CREATE IS TO ENJOY.

You cannot Create in effort; you can Create only in PLEASURE. Every time you are looking for solutions thinking about what to do, you are doing, you are not Creating. When you Create, it is the solution that manifests itself to You. It is not you who are looking for it. When you Create, it is the vital energy that comes to You, the energy recalled by PLEASURE and the Sensuality that you feel in everything.

In every experience you live, ask yourself:

"Am I ENJOYING right now?"

It does not matter what you are doing: it can be eating, sleeping, or writing. The question is: "Am I ENJOYING? DO I FEEL what I live in every one of my cells? Or am I just doing?"

If the response of your consciousness tells you that you are doing, you are not Creating.

Creation is born from PLEASURE, and this is effortless.

Now, Staying in the present Consciousness, observe the

past . . . I am not telling you to enter the past; I am inviting you to observe. OBSERVE.

As a soul every time you chose to go down to Earth, you chose a womb, a home in which to prepare yourself for your coming. You wanted that womb; you did not want another one, You Wanted that Mother and You Wanted that Father to be the masculine of your coming.

NOW, in this instant I invite you to breathe, breathe deeply, let go of all thoughts. Many of them are not yours.

Breathe, let go of the mind that makes you see the conflicts you had with your parents. They are not conflicts; they are evolutionary experiences. The purpose of the FAMILY of ORIGIN is really to help you evolve. It does not matter how it went. It matters now how it goes. When you came down to Earth, You chose them. You wanted those PARENTS, and beyond what Your conception was, You were born from PLEASURE. You were born from ENJOYMENT. You were born from the union and fusion of masculine and feminine energy. The spermatozoon and the egg met, fell in love, united and fused, and ENJOYING themselves, they Created.

ENJOYMENT in Creation is natural.

This is the Eternal Consciousness you need to Create. This is what you need to CREATE.

DOING is born out of fear. CREATING is born out of Trust.

In DOING you use only a part of YOU. In CREATING You are all of YOU.

In DOING you use You. In CREATING you ENJOY YOU.

The essence of the masculine nectar is the spermatozoon, that of the feminine energy is the Crystal cave of the egg.

When these meet they ENJOY; they do not strive.

Everything is natural. Everything is simple. Everything is normal.

Creation is simple.

In CREATION there is no effort.

This is the Consciousness of Creating.

A spermatozoon and an egg that meet ENJOY, not strive. Through the nectar of the masculine energy, the spermatozoon with its Sweet Firmness chooses that egg. It does not want another. Just like the spirit chooses Your soul; it wanted HER, not another. The inherent reception of the ovarian cup was ready to welcome that masculine because that was its masculine; it did not want another. This is what happens within You as well.

Once again I say to you: let go of the fact that you are a man or a woman. You are a DIVINE-HUMAN.

The spermatozoon is the Spirit; the egg is the Soul. The dance of the Masculine and the Feminine began at the origin of Creation. When it began, they enjoyed themselves; they did not strive. Through their ENJOYMENT, they allowed You to experience yourself.

Now, as you read and feel this frequency, breathe it into

Yourself. If you get distracted from the mass consciousness you will say:

"Yes Myriam, but all the experiences in which I suffered so much where do we put them? I could have done without them."

Of course, you could have done without them if you had another consciousness, but the time was not ripe. Now it is. Now You are a nondormant conscious being. Now it is the Time of Your Eternal Consciousness. Now it is the Time you have always waited for.

No past should be repudiated; it should only be alchemically transmuted.

Nothing is destroyed; everything is Transformed.

Every experience you had has been necessary to MAKE YOU who you Are.

The consciousness of DOING is different from the Consciousness of CREATING.

In this moment of deep exploration, what you experience is precious, not harmful. It is a GIFT.

I know you experience moments when tears wet your eyes. Let it happen without getting into the drama. Let your tears bathe you as they did when you were in Your Mother's womb. You were immersed in water, and when you were born, you gushed to life as if from a spring, letting Your beauty shine through.

Everything is natural. Breathe . . . Let it happen. Allow it to happen.

All the experiences you have are just experiences. There are no mistakes in them; there is nothing wrong with them. Whoever judges remains in the consciousness of what is good and right. It is the faded message recorded in some of your old cells that, moment after moment, breath after breath, are continuously renewing themselves. You can be unaware, not guilty.

You are not erasing the old.

You are renewing yourself with NEW CELLS.

You are TRANSMUTING . . .

Look at your face, observe your skin, feel your body of consciousness speaking to you. Let yourself be enlightened by your body of Light that gradually penetrates you passionately, as the Spirit has penetrated your Soul.

As the Fire has penetrated the Water, as the Air has penetrated Earth.

As the spirit has penetrated YOU, because You are SOUL.

You are a talking soul, a playing soul, a laughing soul, a sensually alive soul.

You are the All.

You are the New.

You are Whole.

You are Complete.

Give yourself to You.

SURRENDER YOURSELF to You.

Let yourself GIVE, not help.

Help comes from NEED, and You have to be there to fill yourself with You. There cannot be someone else in your place.

GIVING comes from your ETERNAL CONSCIOUSNESS.

You are not your body, you are not your thoughts, you are not your emotions, you are not energy. You are consciousness. You are who you are with the awareness of being aware.

This is consciousness.

Every word contains a consciousness.

The same word for each of you has a different resonance.

Because each of you had different experiences that gave origin to that word that holds their frequency.

Breathe . . .

Be Kind to You. Be full of GRACE with You.

Be lovingly complicit with Yourself.

No one can do that for you.

Surrender yourself and Give yourself to You.

Soul companion . . .

CREATION IS ENJOYMENT.

Creation is FAST.

Creation happens in an instant and ENJOYS infinity.

It does not matter how long it took You to understand an aspect of You, an experience, the childhood, other lives, and all that you discovered; it does not matter what happened when you become Aware that this was an experience not your condemnation. The CONSCIOUSNESS changes, it transmutes. New Energy comes to You.

The Creation of Consciousness of a New Experience is immediate.

Let go of the old belief system that makes you think you need as much time to integrate your aspects as you did previously, devoting many years to what humans call therapy. The word *therapy* contains an old consciousness. And the old separates you, holds you back.

BREATH, that is what you need.

Compared to before, more and more you find yourself breathing deeply NOW, not because you understand something but because you are allowing yourself to be.

You know that so much can come to you NOW. Open yourself up. Embrace it.

Breathe deeply.

The old goes by itself when it does not feel nurtured.

The Eternal comes to You when it feels desired.

This is the Eternal Consciousness.

This is THE Eternal CONSCIOUSNESS OF ME.

Soul companion . . .

It is indeed much of what is coming.

It is a cyclone of energy made available for You.

It is a tsunami of love that pulls your wings off your body and blows into your heart the distillation of who you are.

With Sweet Firmness, with no procrastination and no more excuses.

Breathe, Breathe, Breathe ancient soul.

Breathe and rest in You.

It is simple. It is really so simple that sometimes it feels weird. Just as simple as the language I use to speak to you through the Ray, so that you can listen.

Everything is simple.

Everything is essential.

Everything is natural.

Simplicity unhinges the gates of the mind.

NOW, it is precisely of the mind that I wish to speak to you.

Breathe . . . breathe and listen . . .

A way to DISTRACT YOURSELF from the soul is to blame someone and often the mind too.

THE MIND is not SEPARATE from YOU.

THE MIND is there and desires YOUR love, as does THE SHADOW.

Stop SEPARATING.

You Are BODY.

You Are MIND.

You Are SPIRIT.

You Are LIGHT.

You Are SHADOW.

You Are CONSCIOUSNESS.

You Are ALL.

How many times do you find yourself saying: "Yes, but my mind . . . "

Or: "It is my rational side . . . It is my mind that makes me believe . . . " Those are excuses. EXCUSES do not mean you are wrong.

You talk about the MIND as if it lives in a separate house from you.

It lives in You. You cannot always blame it. It serves no one.

To point your finger at the mind is to point the finger at You who are also mind.

Mind, lying, are sounds that evoke the Consciousness of the false, which is why you avoid it. A musical refrain that stiffens you for what was, not for what is.

Inside You there is a part that is afraid of being false.

The mind is an instrument that plays through You and for You.

The one who plays it, however, is you; the music is Yours, and it is wonderful as it is.

Soul companion . . .

BE KIND TO YOURSELF. When you truly are, you will not expect others to be kind to you, and as a result, others will naturally be kind to you.

Step out of PRETENSION and enter into PRESENCE.

The Mind is the masculine part of you. And this is not to blame. It must be loved, not criticized.

I return to UNITE with him, not to replace him. This is the first message that I have conveyed to the Ray through which I speak to you.

I return in that part of You that has never allowed itself

to let go. To continue to deny the mind dressed as masculine is to allow it to come back stronger than before.

Let your masculine celebrate.

Celebrate its surrender.

The feminine energy RECEIVES.

The masculine energy is the one that GIVES.

The GIFT comes from the MASCULINE within You, and this is why it must be welcomed, not criticized—just like that spermatozoon that wanted only You.

The union, the eternal androgyny, this You Are.

Not masculine or feminine, but masculine and feminine.

There is no longer separation between the two Forces. The energy is one.

It does not matter if your body is that of a man.

It does not matter if it is that of a woman.

It does not matter if you love a man or a woman or love both.

Love, period!

Love the union of You.

Love the completeness of You.

This is the GIFT.

This is the Creation.

This is to Create.

The Eternal Consciousness of the word ENJOY is GOD in all eras.

This is the essence of You.

I love you soul companion. I love you deeply.

IN THE AKASHIC ROOMS

In the Sacred Silence a music is heard. It touches the soul. It is Intense. It is Passionate. It is Strong. It vibrates and becomes deeper. It seems to dig into the bowels of centuries where the truth of Human history becomes more and more crystalline.

The musical notes pound, the ardent rhythm of the heart throbs, the passion pulses, and the loquacious silence shines through the depths of the raven eyes of the two who, two thousand years later, unite in the TRUTH of their love.

He wears an ecru light linen dress. He is dark in the eyes, amber in the skin; the soft waves of his hair frame the oval of his face. She is enchanting, beautiful, dressed in her innocence, wearing a soft white silk dress edged with gold, sensual and delicate. In her hand is a bundle of white roses with one red rose that stands out in the center, the symbol of the burning passion of the soul that asks to love.

The wedding march penetrates the soul of those who have always waited for their Union. Everything is ready to celebrate the Cosmic Wedding. The altar is an ancient *menhir,* the carpets are made of flowers, the benches of almond, pine, and walnut wood.

SHE, clothed in her transparent beauty as her very soul, is completely naked under her dress. In the center of her chest is the *key to life*. Her heart is Innocent, and the truth of her Mastery now throbs with the New Frequency.

Joy is proud to be among the first to be invited, elegant,

dressed to party in his sea-blue suit. He is excited, smiles and cries with joy.

The Parents of the bride and groom present in their essence left a gift for them: two precious CROWNS set with crimson-colored crystals and sapphires. They are all there: Her friends, one of whom is very dear to the Bride, her name is Salome, another Martha, and many of His friends, Joseph, James, Philip. . . . There are twelve of them.

Life after life, experience after experience, here they are now together celebrating the *truth* of the Cosmic Couple. The alchemical Marriage is ready to be experienced.

Other guests arrive from all ages: free Cathars with no more vows of penance; Templars on white horses, proud of their rediscovered truth; others still surrendered to the evidence of the facts revealed by the centuries. All have their faces uncovered; no headgear covers their heads. Their hearts burn with the fire of Love and no longer with the stake of injustice.

Everyone has already lived through every experience of victim and executioner, and in the last Time lives his Royal Mastery, recognizing himself in the same substance of the Universal Creation. It is no longer time to feel guilty. Everything was written in the Divine Script.

Behind the altar is Peter. It is Him, the guest of honor. It is Him, the witness surrendered to love. It is Him, who will begin the ceremony. It is Him, who before consecrating the timeless moment of union and love, with a modest face, walks toward Myriam, with love and respect, kneeling down, kisses her feet, which at that moment are illuminated by a ray of sunlight and adorned with golden sandals on which small fragments of ruby are set. Peter looks into the depths of Myriam's eyes. He cries, he cries sobbing, salt water flows from his eyes, a sea of emotions and feelings ripple through his aching heart.

She, with a nod of sacred respect and deep empathy, offers him her strong and delicate hand and invites him to stand up.

Peter is amazed; he cannot believe his eyes. He feared that Myriam was bitter toward Him for his past behavior and that she had a desire for revenge against him.

Myriam, centered in her Heart and in the completeness of herself, welcomes Peter into her arms, and he who hated women, unaware of hating his own feminine part, in front of so much Love and pure compassion, is deeply moved and with his own tears clears up his old fears. He expands his Consciousness and in his rhythmic breathing becomes aware that Myriam no longer represents a Feminine to be jealous of or to fight nor even to fear.

Peter feels the love growing for himself. Centuries of past lives dissolve in the atmosphere of an Eternal Consciousness. His wound no longer hurts, healed by love like a sun, which expands, radiating him with the New Frequency.

He knows that in the New Time he cannot put aside his pain by pretending to be strong. He cannot force himself to be a HERO. He can no longer fight a war to seek the recognition of a medal. He cannot, but above all he no longer wants to. His masculine surrenders. He surrenders to self-love. He surrenders to his heart, which has always suffered from the NEED TO BE RECOGNIZED and accepted by the Great Mother, by the Woman.

The wound in his heart, thanks to Myriam's Love and Sweet Firmness, is healed.

Myriam's welcoming energy allowed him to abandon himself to trust and to lovingly take care of his heart. A humble masculine that asks forgiveness from his own heart, from his inner woman, from his creativity, from his soul, from Myriam, and "*in the name of the ROSE,*" from all WOMEN.

Peter, confident and no longer afraid of being judged, turns in the Here and Now to the feminine energy. Now he knows that she, Myriam, the Woman, is not outside. She is the mirror of his Creative Power, of his capacity to welcome himself. Now he knows that with Self-love, every woman can heal the wound of her *womb* and every man can heal the wound of his *heart*.

The Masculine and Feminine make love in the GRAIL of the Human Angel and in the nectar of experience merge into one Energy: L O V E . . .

The love that is neither male nor female.

The love that, like the soul, simply IS.

Myriam with Sweet Firmness invites Peter to listen to his

feminine side, and in that instant he hears a reassuring voice speaking to him inside:

"I love you, Peter! I am You. I cannot do anything other than welcome you and love you, because You are Me."

A priestess dressed in white appears next to Peter. She is his new companion, ready to love him. Peter has learned to love HIMSELF and to love the Woman, first of all his own, the inner one, the welcoming part of himself with which Myriam has welcomed the masculine and reflected it. Now everything is crystal clear, transparent. Golden dust blown by the wind rests lightly on the heads of all the jubilant, joyful guests aware of their Eternal Consciousness.

Crystalline children flow among the guests like gushing water, sparkle with smiles, handing out Magdala-flavored almond candies.

The Celebration begins with the Rite of Flowers. Myriam, enchanting and innocent in her candor, has before her timeless eyes a veil of rosy organza that lets the antiquity of her soul shine through. Her auburn hair rests on her shoulders, and soft curls lie on the soft skin of her tumescent breasts.

He looks at her for a long time, speaking only with his breath, gently uncovers her face, while the frame of silence is the music with which the Rite begins.

Joy's heart beats, aware that he has been waiting for this moment forever.

Like a film, Joy looks back at the countless times he has

wished to see Yeshua and Myriam UNITED in love on all altars. *"Man dare not separate what God has united."* Only now does Joy understand the essence of those words. He remembers all the moments when someone in front of that cross made him believe he was guilty. He remembers lived experiences, and he hears echoes of distant voices from a very faded time. He is aware that no one is guilty and that, except for himself, there is no one from whom to ask forgiveness. He understands that he himself is the Gift, and through it he Finds himself and Loves himself.

Joy exudes Joy. Every pore of his skin is a bursting sun of rediscovered love. His every organ is a volcano throbbing with passion. His blood is Crystal Clear Water flowing. His eyes are beacons illuminating life.

He continues to revel in what he can see through the eyes of his soul.

Myriam lets her Beloved look at her for a long time, and he gently places his left hand on her chest, feeling her heart. She, feeling touched in her soul, makes the same gesture toward him, who smiles at her. They nod with their eyes, accomplices of an ancient PROMISE. Their eyes speak of ancient love. Tears wet their faces creating a faint pathway that flows straight to the Cup of the Heart. Here is the Holy Grail.

Both quench their thirst from the nectar of their own souls and in the self-love share the love for and of each other. The *distillate* of the experience becomes a drop of the sea that in the tears of both flows freely.

"Here is my Beloved. Here is my Bride. Here is my Myriam.

The day I left my body You were the beloved. It was Your eyes that saw, for only the soul can see. And this is what You represent. To You I left my word, and in the heart I blew my breath, remember?"

"Of course, My Beloved," Myriam answers with a calm and quiet voice, without ever taking her eyes off him.

"I told you that many lives would await you.

And many TRIALS you would face.

So it was, my beloved Yeshua.

I have looked for you and felt you in every man. I have looked for you and felt you in every life."

"I have looked for you in every woman," Yeshua adds, feeling ever more strongly the warmth of Myriam's hand on his chest, now surrendered to Her.

"Do you remember? I told you that it would have taken two millennia before humanity surrendered to its own Creative Power. I told you that in the Name of the Mother in the New Time, Life would be celebrated. Now is that Time! Now is the Time of the Eternal Consciousness of You.

Myriam, my beloved. Great Mother, my Sophia. I have always loved you and never forgotten you. I am You and You are Me, my beloved. Your sweet strength is now here to be Honored, Consecrated, Recognized, and Loved in the name of the Rose.

The rose has the fragrance of the soul.

The rose has the frequency of love.

The rose has the frequency of union."

Amid smiles, songs, and rose petals, a couple of children with particularly blue and transparent eyes arrive, giving them two roses, one intensely red and the other candidly white. There are no rings and no handfasting, no signatures and no contracts.

ONLY LOVE.

The young and ancient Master Souls joyfully bring the bride and groom's attention to two soft cushions made of lily petals. The Gifts of their Parents, eternally present within their essence, are ready to be worn. Each one recognizes his or her royal Mastery, and uniting themselves and mirroring in the eyes of the other, they recognize themselves by becoming One.

"I return to unite with him, not to replace him," she joyfully states. Directing her gaze to the guests, she observes them and recognizes them all as integral parts of herself. Pieces of Crystal united and firm in the memory of her Eternal Consciousness.

"Here beside my Bridegroom. Here beside my King.
Here beside my Beloved, I Return to Unite myself."

Yeshua looks at her, smiles, caresses her cheek, touches her delicate and soft lips, looks at her again in the depths of her gaze, and floods her with Passion with a deep kiss on her mouth.

Their breaths unify. The motions of their hearts sway and like tides alternate in the naturalness of their bodies imbued with love.

From symbiosis to one, in a sacred dance the Flesh becomes Spirit, canceling every separation.

The Masculine ENJOYS its Feminine, and the Feminine allows itself to Be in the Masculine. The Sacred Androgyny breathes in the One.

No limits. No boundaries. No identification.

ONLY LOVE.

Their physical and ethereal bodies breathe in unison, intertwining in the emphasis of pure love. The passion of the bodies in the Bridal Chamber burns with Intimate and Ancient Knowledge.

Everything is pure; everything is candid. Nothing is sinful. She lets herself be penetrated by the seed of love. Her soft skin smells of Divine essence. Her scent of myrrh burns in the auras of their silver and gold energies. Her auburn hair caresses his chest, and the COSMIC COUPLE United by love explodes into the Divine Orgasm, allowing themselves to feel HUMAN PASSION.

"In my Chalice I welcome You.

Fragments of Crystal in me are reunited.

In Your living eyes burns the memory of Eternal Passion.

Sacred honey is Your ointment, and my body, penetrated by love, Gives itself completely to You.

Raven black helices streaked by copper threads touch the infinite instant of Your amber skin.

Ancient mysteries awaken.

Archaic breaths return.

And the ever more vivid memory of times already lived . . .
in the name of the Rose is revealed.
I love you Yeshua."
"I love you too my beloved Myriam."

The *Hieros Gamos* becomes music, and the echo of UNION spreads into the multidimensionality of infinite worlds.

Joy exults, sweats, shakes with passion.

An invisible hand suddenly brushes his face. He wakes up.

He realizes he has been dreaming . . .

He cries, he cries loudly. He cannot explain what has happened to him.

Inside him he feels that on other levels the Cosmic Marriage has taken place. He feels the UNION within himself. He feels the love of his sensual Masculine and the delicacy of the Feminine. He lets them dance in the Golden Tabernacle of his heart, while in the distance the light of Yeshua and Myriam reflects the rediscovered Cosmic Couple within himself. He tries to reach them, runs, takes a long breath, and stops. He understands that it is no longer time to run, that it is no longer time to toil to seek outside what is already inside. He realizes that he himself is Pure Light. The shadow has stopped frightening him; it is now his faithful companion, his accomplice and no longer his rival.

Joy feels at Home. He is Aware that he himself is a couple and a cup of his own Unity. He closes his eyes, and like a Mother when she takes her newborn baby to her breast, he takes his heart in his arms. He loves it, thanks it, honors it, and with his Eternal Consciousness Consecrates it.

His heart speaks to him of the love it feels for him . . .

"*I love you, Joy,*" it tells him.

"*You, male in body and female in name, have sought me everywhere and in everyone . . . it does not matter if you have sometimes forgotten me. I love You and I have never judged you . . . I desire you, Joy. I accept You and I love You as You Are. I want You. I love you, Joy. I love you.*"

A cosmic voice vehemently cries out his name.

"*I love you . . .*

I love you deeply Joy.

Now You Know . . .

Now You Are!

Joy . . . You are Home!

Complete with You, now you Are at Home."

"But who are You? I know You!"

"*I am Your Soul, Joy . . .*

Your Soul."

In the name of the Rose, so it is.

My womb is the Holy Grail
filled with the nectar
of my Sacred Essence.
My womb
is Fire that warms.
My womb
is Water that overflows.
My womb
is red Earth that pulses.
My womb
is Breath that breathes.
My womb
is the temple of archaic mysteries.
My womb is the bridge chosen by the soul
that calls me Mother.
My womb is the sacred way
that accompanies my beloved to God.
My womb is the Sacred Space
where silence becomes poetry.

I dedicate this poem to the womb of the GREAT MOTHER.
The black womb from which everything had its Origin.

ADELE VENNERI

Acknowledgments

The first thanks goes to Joy who, through this initiatory journey, has allowed himself to meet his soul. A soul always sought and never embodied. A journey for and to oneself.

A heartfelt thanks goes to Gian Marco Bragadin, writer and former editor of the Melchidesek publishing house. A gentleman of other times, in which grace and intelligence merge into a unique soul.

I would like to thank all those who have participated in all the experiential holidays that, since 2011, I have organized in different places of high vibratory frequency. Places where, accompanied by the Myriam Frequency, all those who have chosen to be there have allowed themselves to discover their own soul potentials, thus accessing other levels of consciousness. From France to Iceland, from the island of Montecristo to the holy mountain of Montserrat, from Saintes-Maries-de-la-Mer to Rennes-le-Château, from the unknown to the known self.

A very special thanks goes to Susanna Memoli, the one who, with infinite love, has translated this book. I first met her in France, in Alet-les-Bains, on the occasion of a celebration dedicated to Mary Magdalene, which I had organized for July 22, 2019. In the ritual, the water flowed fluidly just as her tears fell from her eyes. As an anthropologist, Susanna had done much research on the Mother Goddess and on the sacred feminine, but it was in that look between us that she recognized herself as the essence of what she had always sought. Since then, not only has she never stopped experiencing the events I organize in Italy and abroad, but she has also become the personal translator of my works, as well as a reference point for my events in Switzerland. Her total dedication has been crucial. This book could have not been translated by someone who only knows the language; it needed someone like Susanna, who also has had concrete experience of what is written in an alchemical way. Grateful, deeply grateful.

A heartfelt thanks to Tori Norah Milner, a young blue-eyed soul, born in Israel in Jerusalem. Tori met me in France, in Alet-les-Bains, in the house where her family manages a marvelous B&B, a place where as soon as you arrive you feel at home. In this oasis of peace I have brought many groups from all over the world, and it is here that we met many times. Since English is her mother tongue, Tori has reread the work translated by Susanna Memoli and edited some of the details.

A special thanks to my son, Stefano Scrimieri, for his constant presence. His anthropological spirit and gratitude toward life have always pushed him to seek the mystery of the human being in all its facets. Here we met, and together we continue our journey.

Through the conclusion of this book, you may believe that your experience ends here, but in reality it has just begun. I thank you already for what you will make of this book. I am sure that you will read it again and again, and each time you will find it different. In fact, it will be your consciousness that will be changed, and each time you will be ready to receive *other*. Thank you for your enthusiasm in spreading it.

Thanks to everyone, but above all thanks to YOU who, through Joy, will experience your journey.

You are *Joy*.